An Affair of Flowers

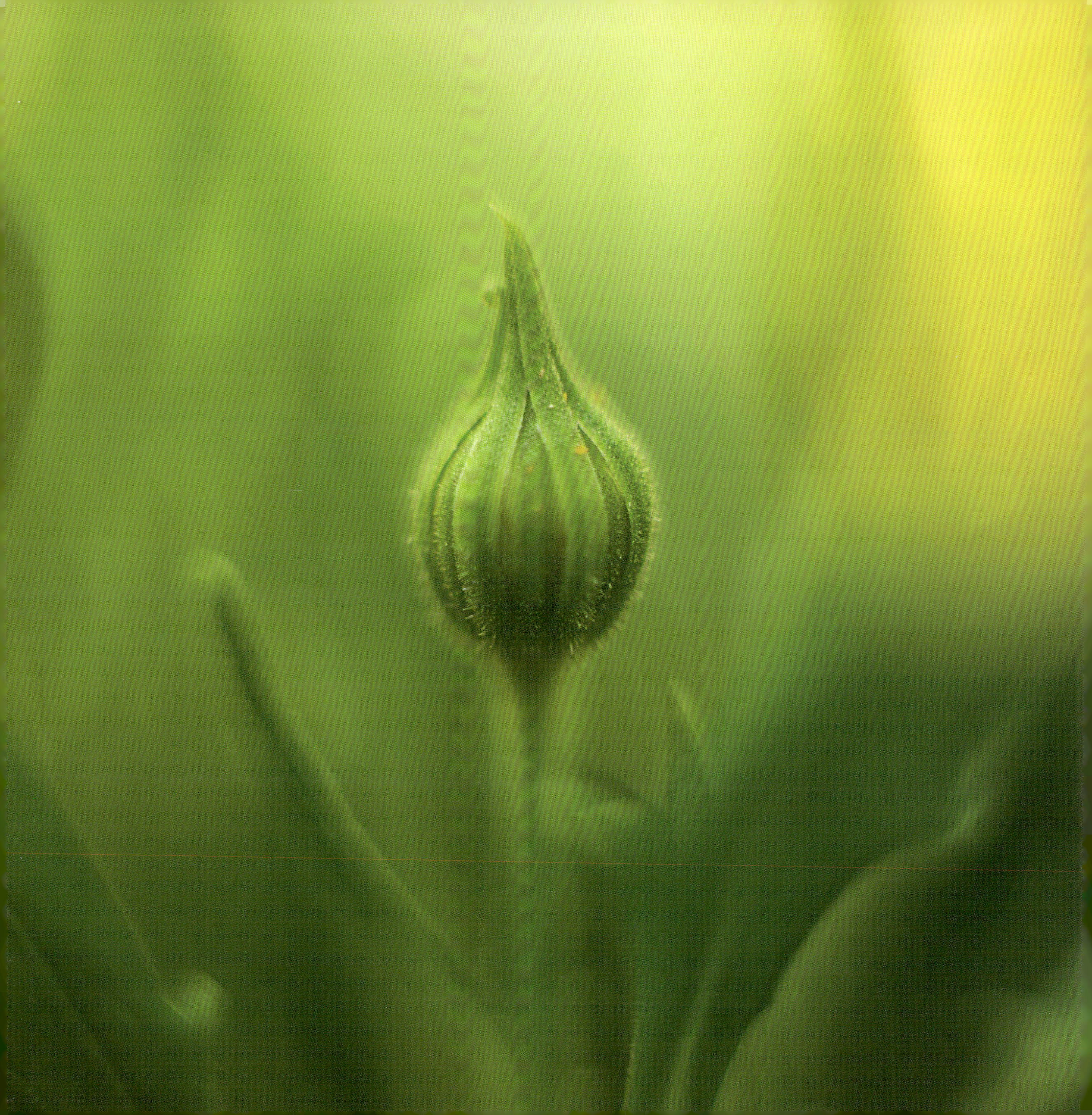

An Affair of Flowers

Photographs by John Robert Rodrigues

Poetry by Patricia Z. Smith

Introduction by Stephen Buchmann

Goff Books

Novato, California

Goff Books

Published by Goff Books. An Imprint of ORO Editions
Gordon Goff: Publisher

www.goffbooks.com
info@goffbooks.com

Photographs by John Rodrigues
Poems by Patricia Z. Smith
Book Design by Tom Walker
Book Design edited by Kirby Anderson
Goff Books Managing Editor, Kirby Anderson

10 9 8 7 6 5 4 3 2 1 First Edition

ISBN: 978-1-954081-72-7

Color Separations and Printing: ORO Group Ltd.
Printed in China.

Goff Books makes a continuous effort to minimize the overall carbon footprint of its publications. As part of this goal, Goff Books, in association with Global ReLeaf, arranges to plant trees to replace those used in the manufacturing of the paper produced for its books. Global ReLeaf is an international campaign run by American Forests, one of the world's oldest nonprofit conservation organizations. Global ReLeaf is American Forests' education and action program that helps individuals, organizations, agencies, and corporations improve the local and global environment by planting and caring for trees.

Dedicated to my wife Debbie and my three children,
Ryan, Michael, and Ashley.

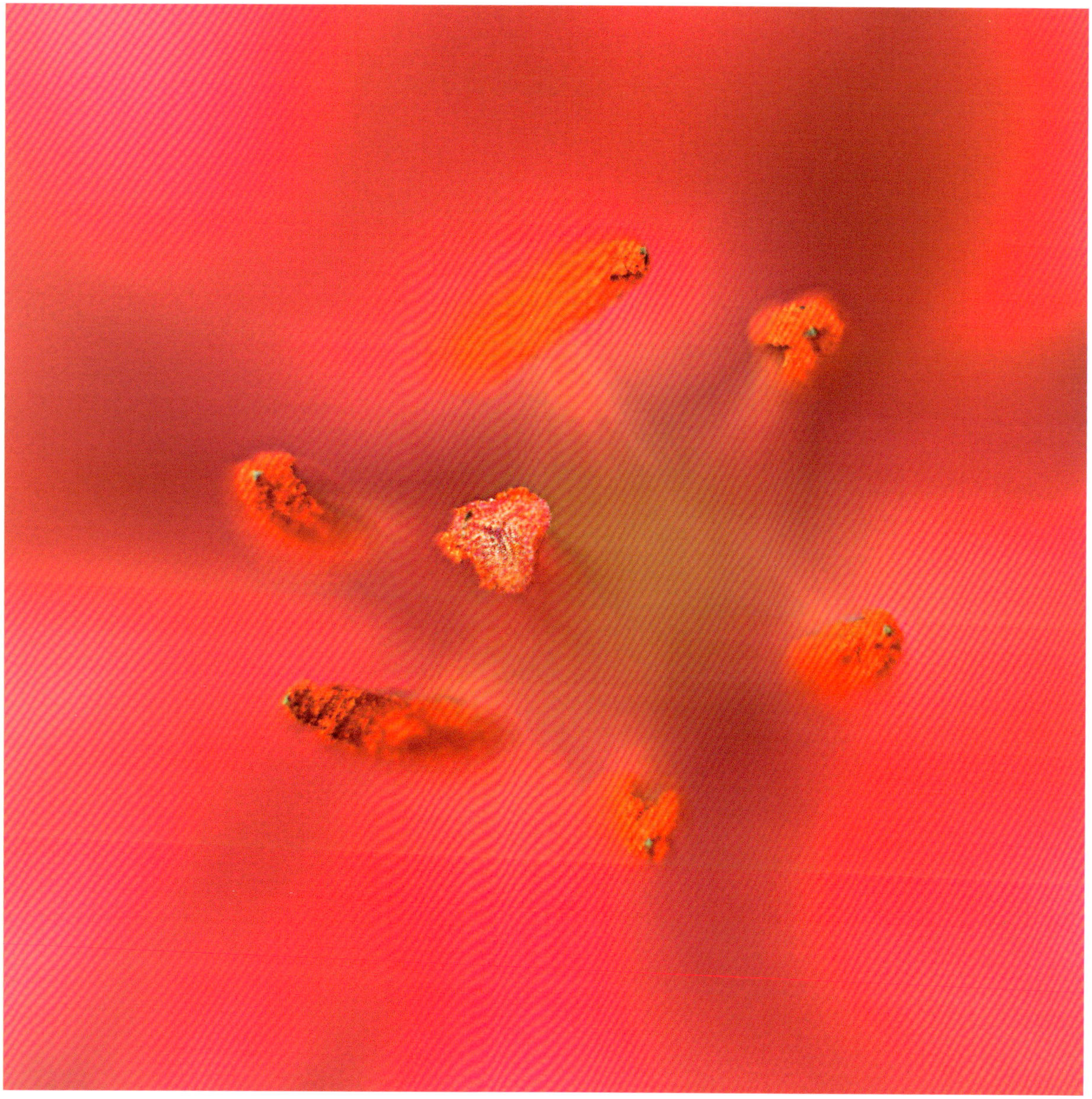

INTRODUCTION

Stephen L. Buchmann

Plants bear flowers for one reason only: Sex. Colorful petals encircle hidden sexual organs, pollen-containing anthers and ovules (future seeds) within fleshy ovaries. Flowers are plant sexual signposts, living billboards, advertising their sweet nectar droplets and nutritious pollen for their visitors. Sniffing a flower brings you close to floral sexual parts.

What are flowers to us? Flowers have been nature's fragrant muses for generations of artists, photographers, and poets. Their myriad shapes, colors, and evocative scents speak to us, making us smile, and enriching our lives. For millennia, flowers have accompanied us from cradle to grave. They remain potent symbols of love, achievement, victory, life, and death.

But what are flowers, actually? Well, they did not evolve for our eyes—to catch our attention. Around 134 million years ago in the Cretaceous forests, browsed by herbivorous dinosaurs, this early evolutionary experiment—the diversification of flowers—began.

Unlike us, flowering plants can't uproot themselves and go on a date. Instead, they signal others for help. Pollinators—insects and animals—are the sexual go-betweens, moving "sperm" (pollen's male gametes) for their immobile partners, from anthers to stigmas. Pollination, an essential service of nature, is followed by fertilization, and then seeds develop within fruits.

Eighty percent of flowering plants rely on animal pollinators (bees, wasps, flies, beetles, butterflies, moths, bats, birds). Most of these conjugal visits are made by the world's 20,000 kinds of bees.

Flowers, and the fruits they become, are essential sustainable resources for humans and wildlife. Floral rewards (pollen, nectar) and nutritious fruits and seeds feed many of the world's animals. Red and orange berries are greedily gulped down by birds and mammals. Wintering bears grow fat on them and hibernate.

Some flowers, nondescript and greenish, cast their fate to the wind—pollen grains caught in the feathery embrace of grass flower stigmas. And these unnoticed events produce the cereal grains—including corn, rice, and wheat—that feed most of the world's 7.5 billion souls. Around the world, 1,400 crop plants that feed humanity begin as flowers, seeds, and fruits.

Flowering plants clothe a verdant world and exhale the very oxygen we breathe. Imagine a world without flowers? Our terrestrial world would have been an impoverished drab brown place without flowering plants. Further, since our hominin ancestors likely depended upon wild fruits and nuts, our own species may never have evolved without the bounty and beauty of flowers. Georgia O'Keefe reminded us that nobody sees a flower really; they are so small. We are too rushed, and seeing takes time—just as it takes time and effort to know a friend, so it is with flowers.

You will get to know flowers with this impressive book! It is richly illustrated with dozens of gorgeous macro flower photographs and also some of their pollinators. John Rodrigues is an artist who has taken that time to truly see. I invite you to sit back, maybe with a cup of hot Chamomile tea, and indulge in these images—taking the time to truly see these flowers, and their winged visitors, and to appreciate their inherent majesty.

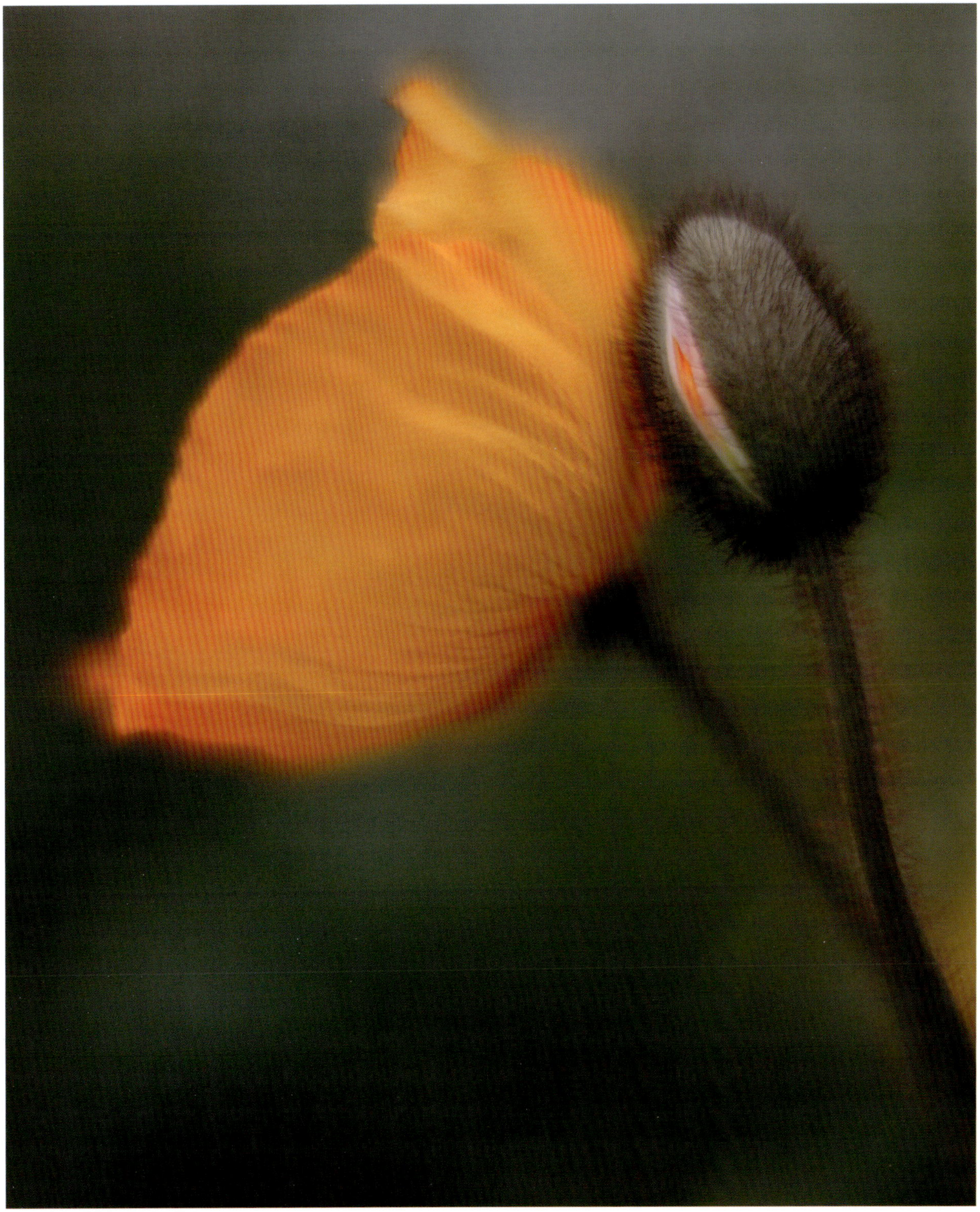

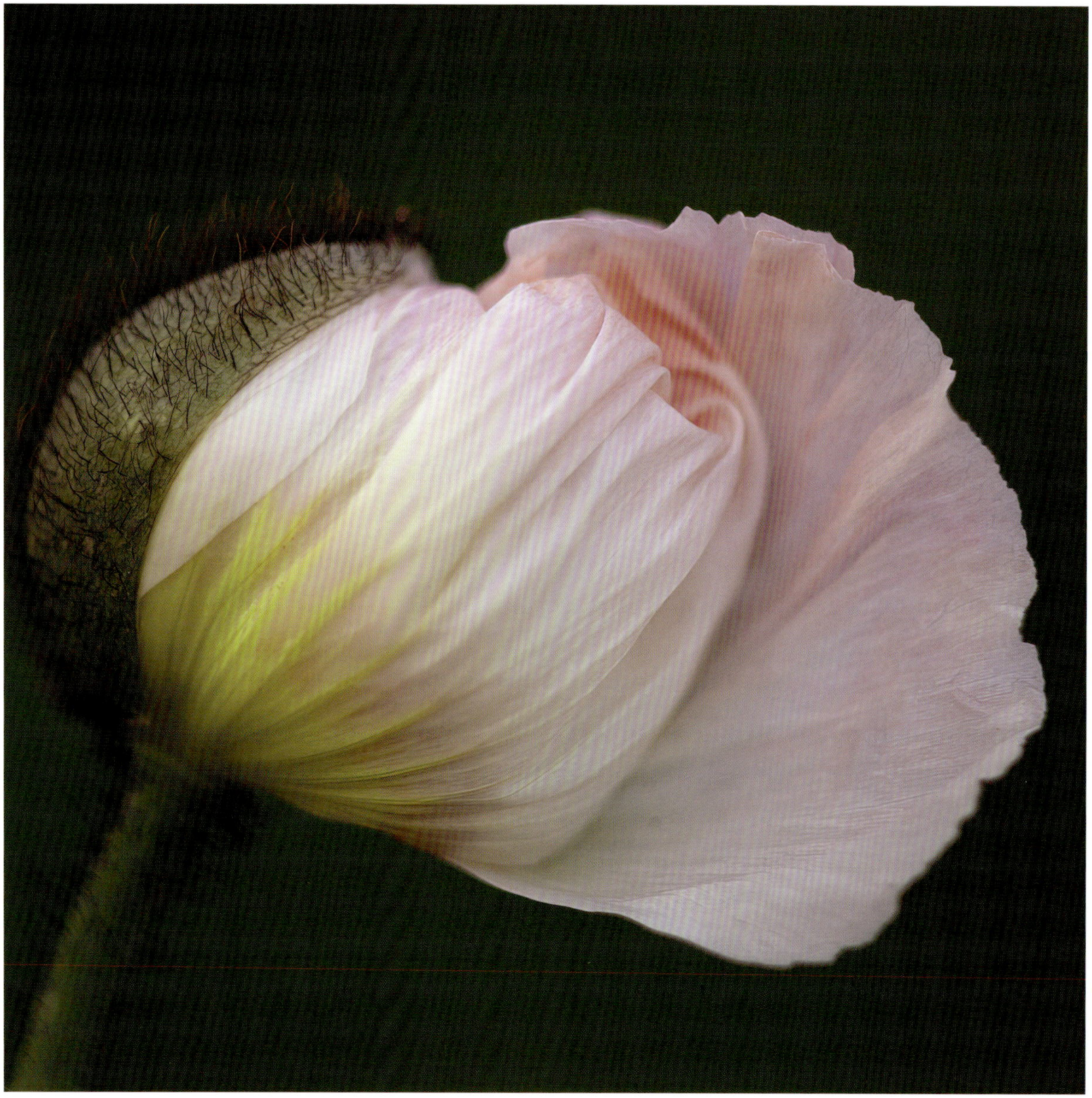

"If we could see the miracle of a single flower clearly our whole life would change."

— Buddha

THE AFFAIRS OF BEES

Bees have made honey from nectar for at least 30 million years.

Honey bee queens (Apis mellifera) lay 1,000 to 2,000 eggs a day, are constantly fed and tended, and can live five years, though two to three years is typical before a queen starts to lose vigor—dying within five to six years—from fulfilling the one item on her job description.

Worker bees are female and typically live five to six weeks. Drones are male and hang out in the hive doing next to nothing, and die within 60 days.

During spring and summer foraging seasons a worker bee flies 20-30 miles per day at a full out flight speed of 15-20 miles per hour, slowing down to visit 2,000-3,000 flowers per day.

A single worker bee gathers enough nectar over Its lifetime to produce approximately 1/12 of a teaspoon of honey.

A good hive clocks in 55,000 to 60,000 flight miles to make a pound of honey.

Best plants for bees are bee balm, sunflowers, phacelia, milkweed, coneflowers, black-eyed susans, alyssum, geraniums, anise hyssop, clover.

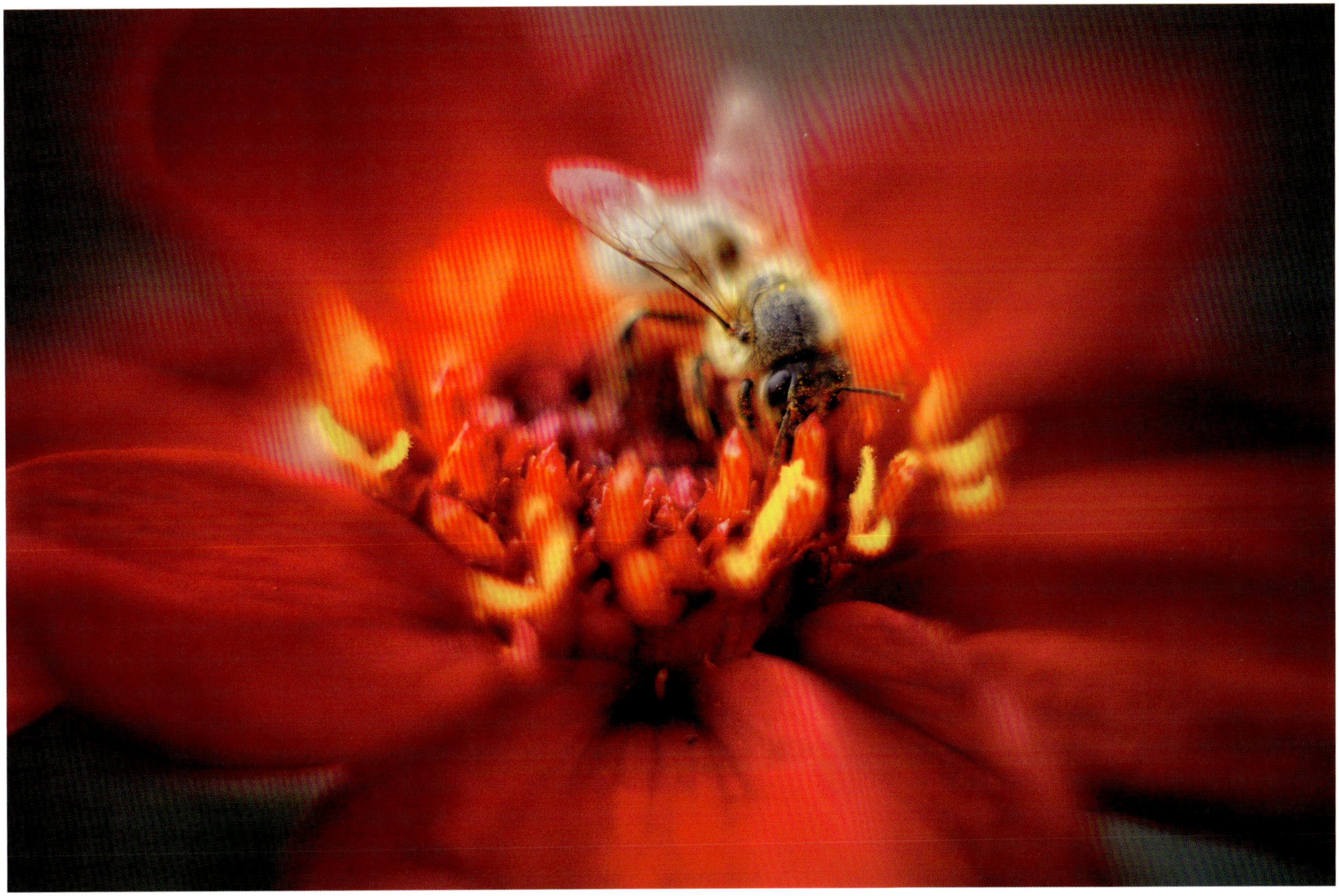

Warm waters and boundless oxygen
gave primordial lagoons options.

Nature, Curiosity Incarnate,
chose enticing sex organs
for her water-logged greenery.

Flaunting, floating, undulating,
first flowers diverged and proliferated
as small mammals made ready
for an asteroid.

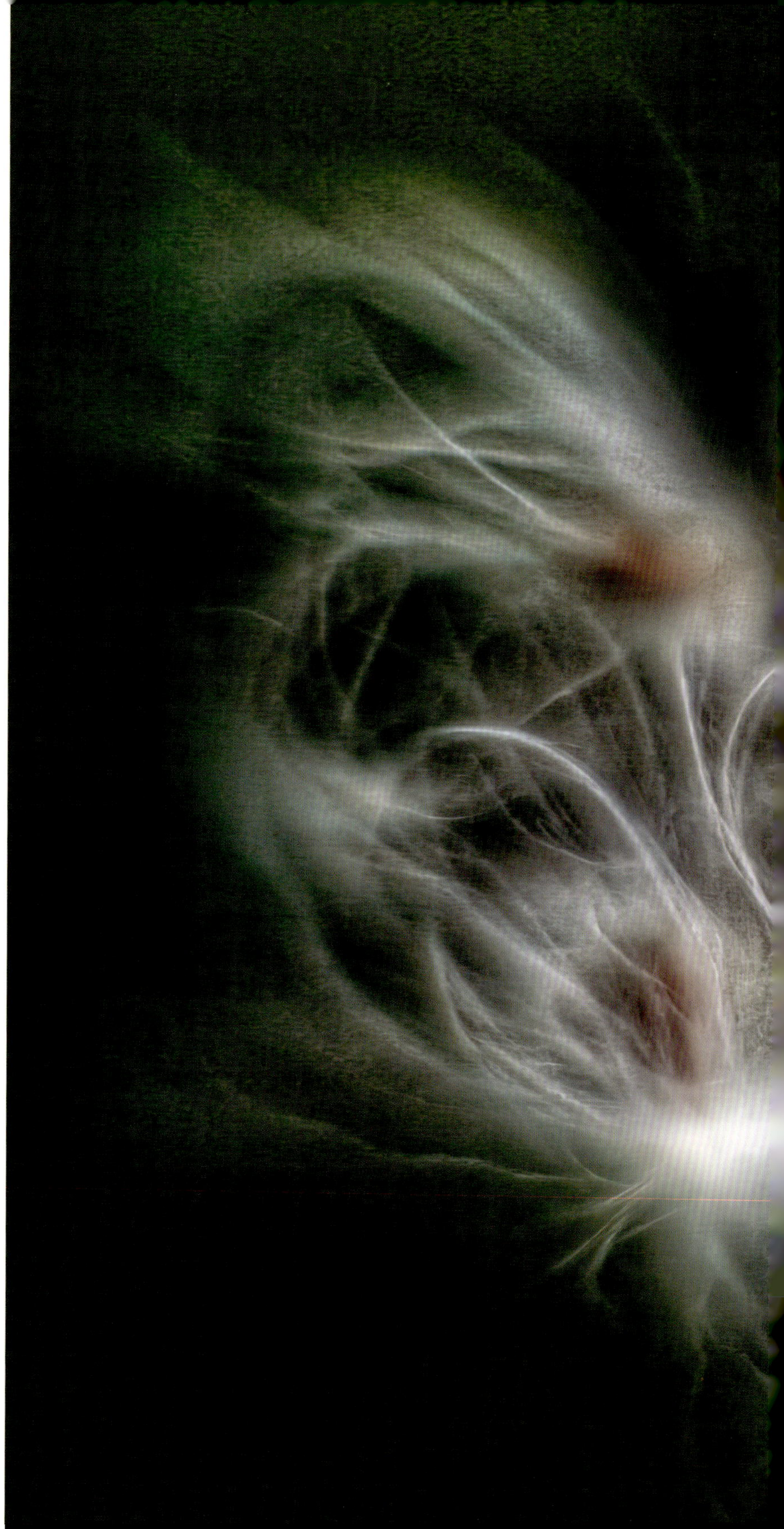

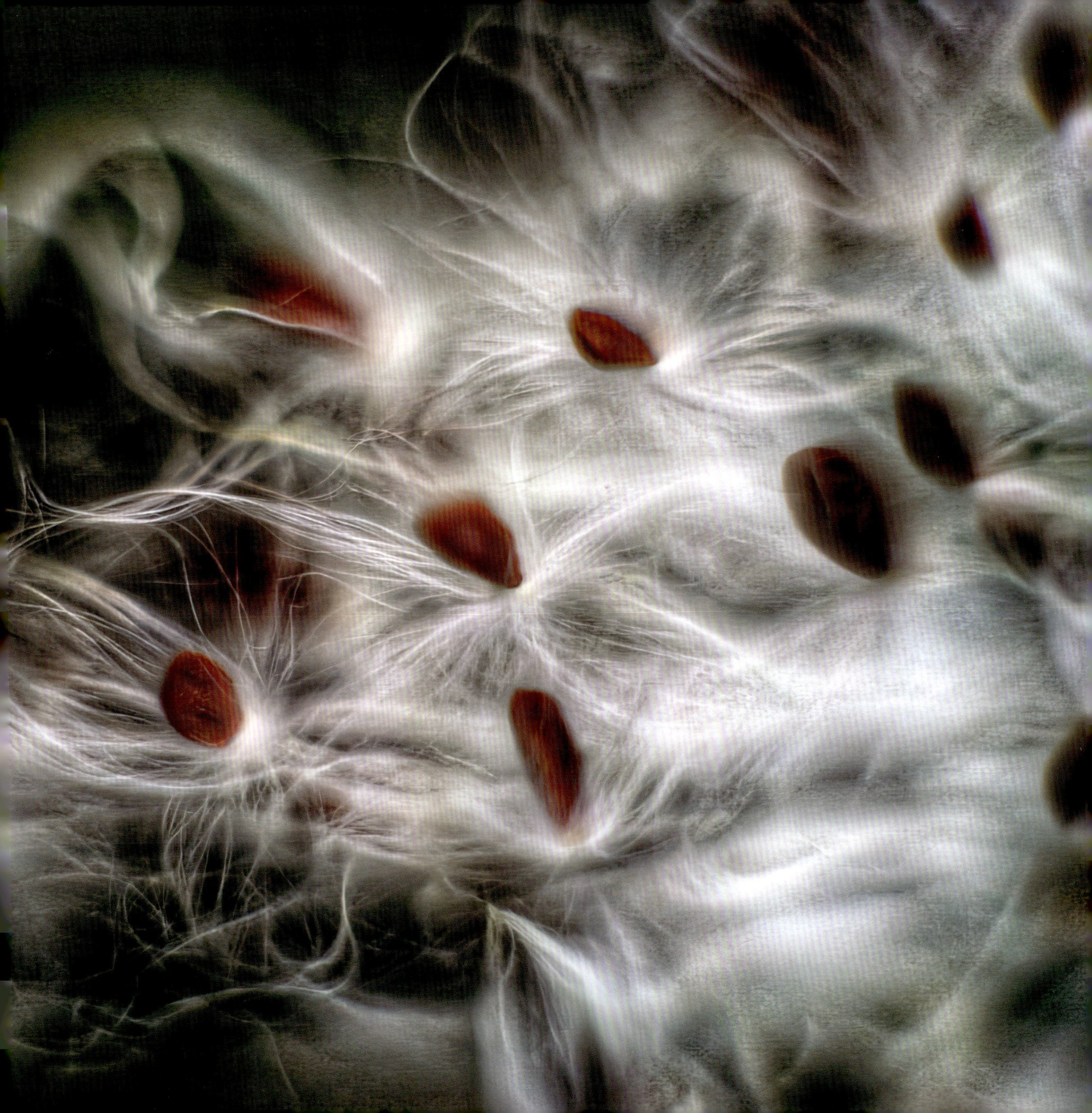

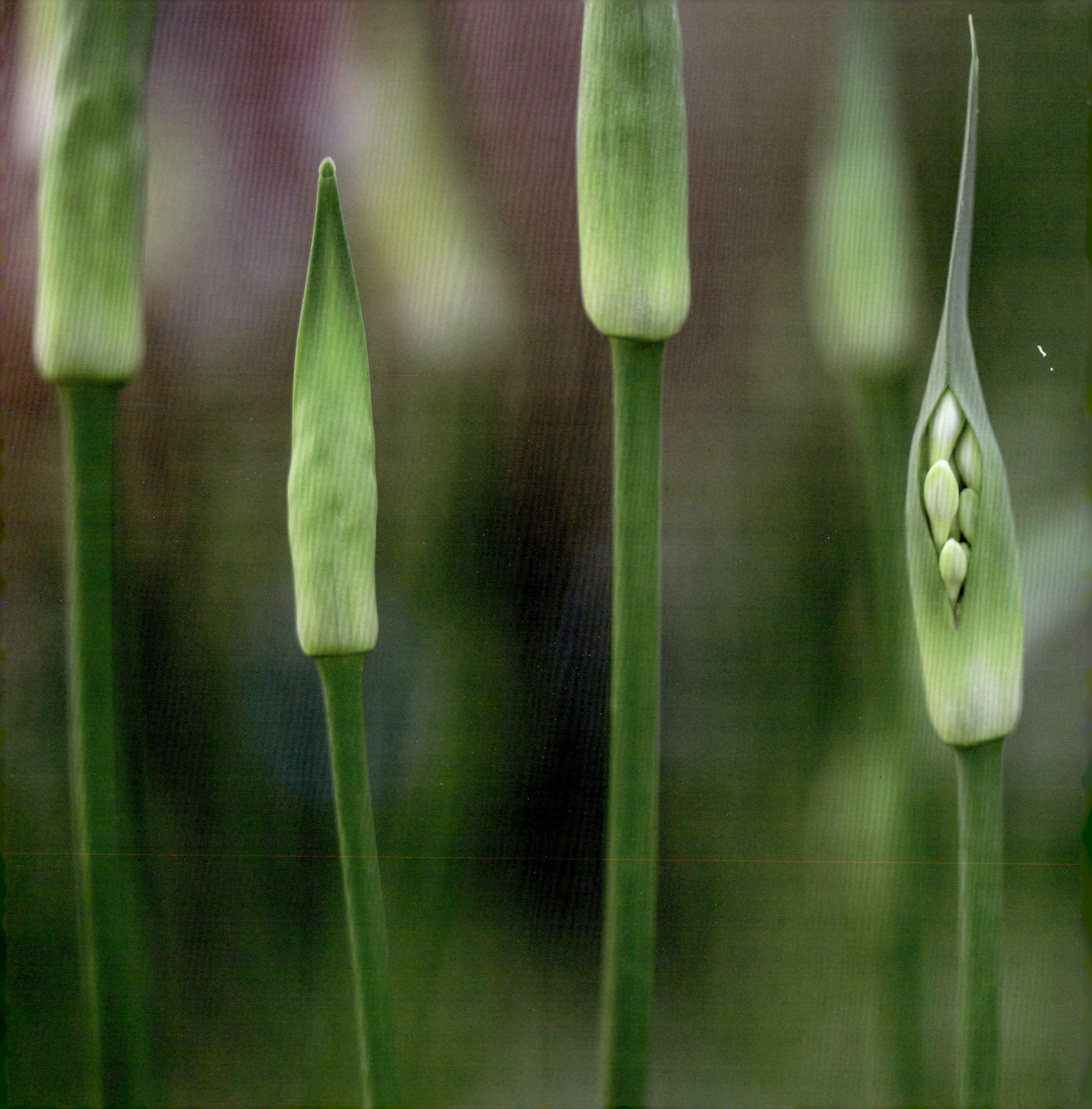

First flowering plants (angiosperms) evolved
during greenhouse climes of the Cretaceous period
around 135 million years ago.

Two to three millimeters across, they were perfect
for the tiny bees and other pollinators.

Now, more than 300,000 species of flowering plants
serve:
    insects with needs
    reptiles with schemes
    mammals making their babies milk
    lovers swooning
    dreamers adrift
    poets despairing
    farmers planting
    grievers grieving
    celebrators celebrating
    perfumeries

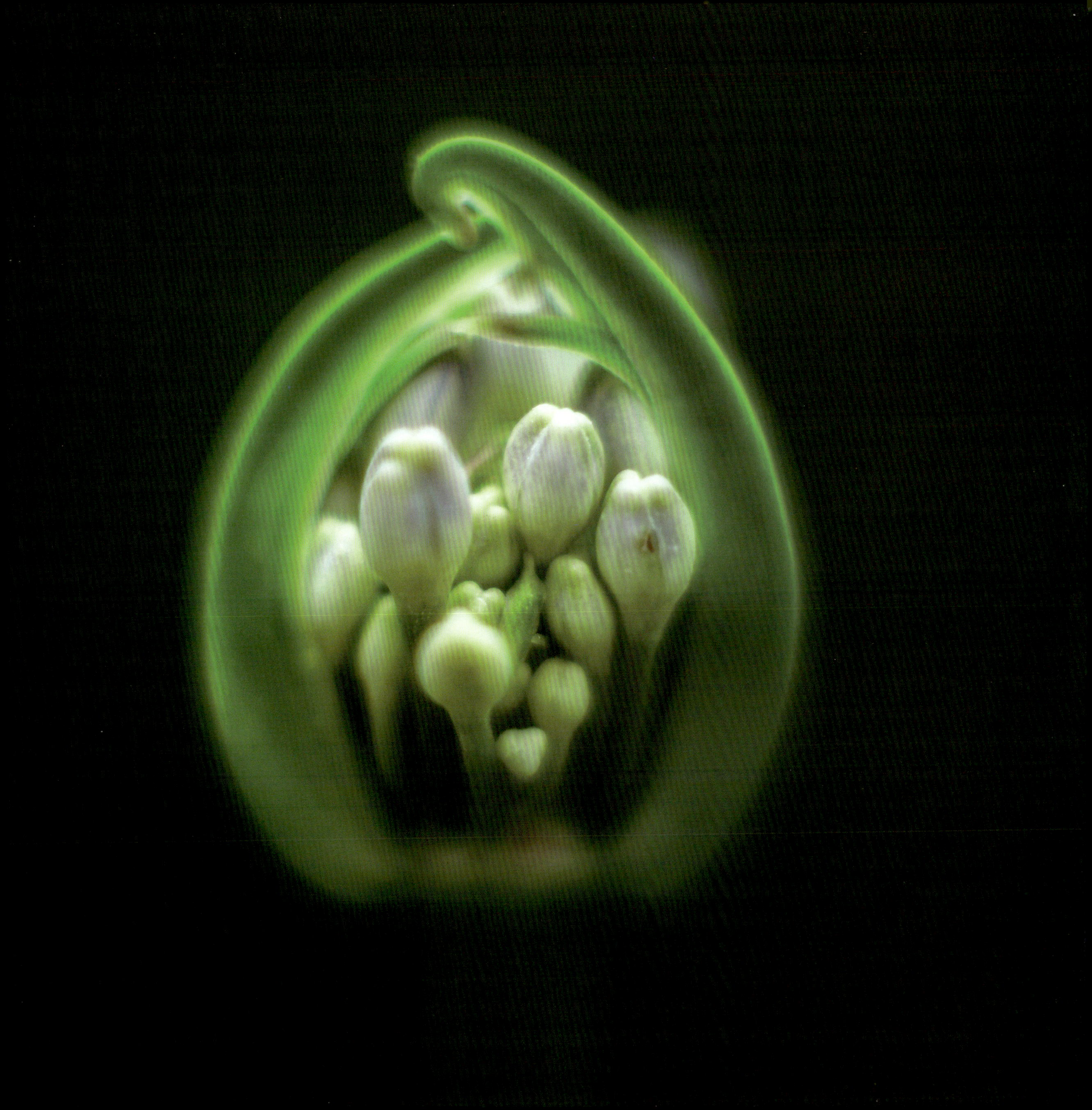

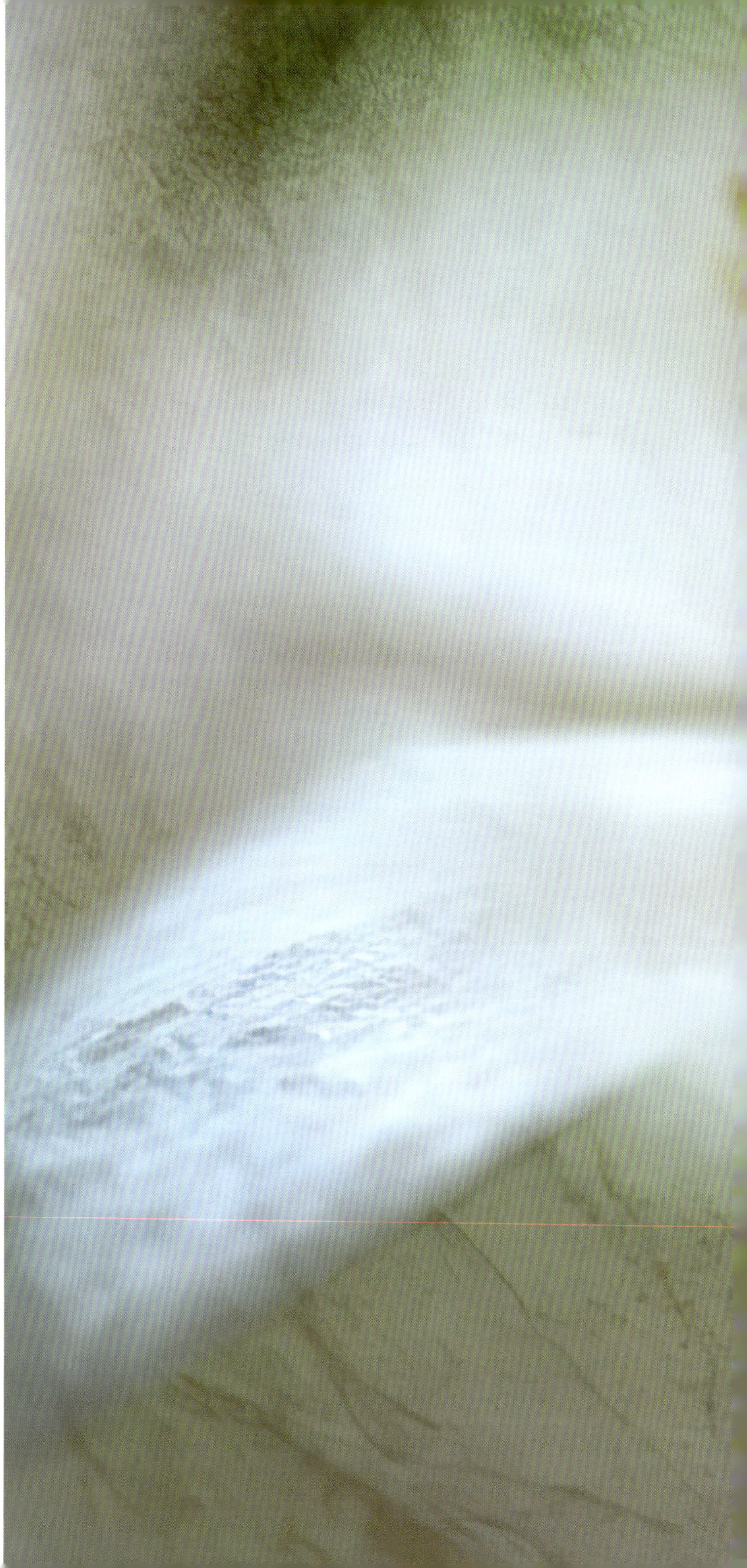

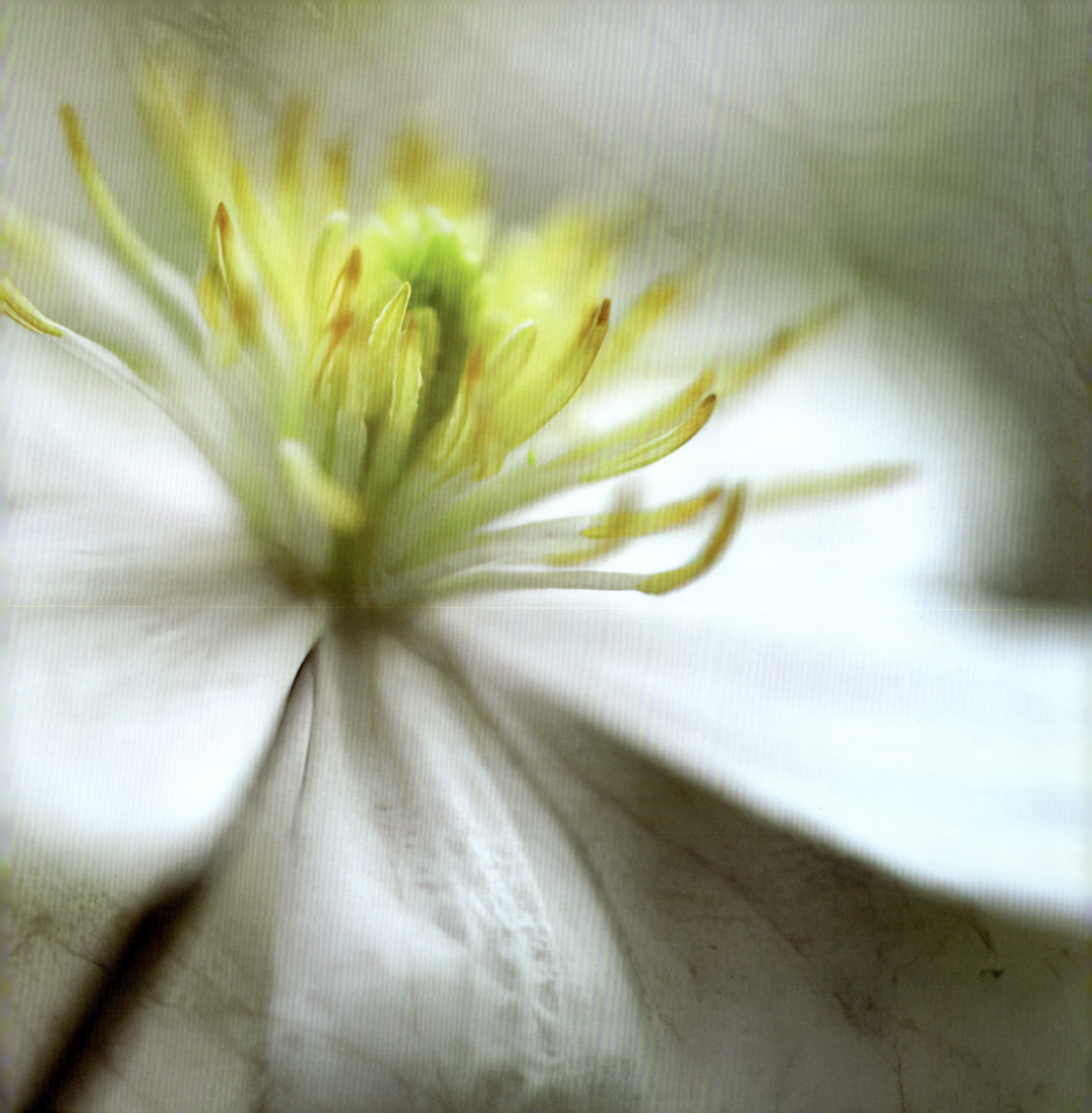

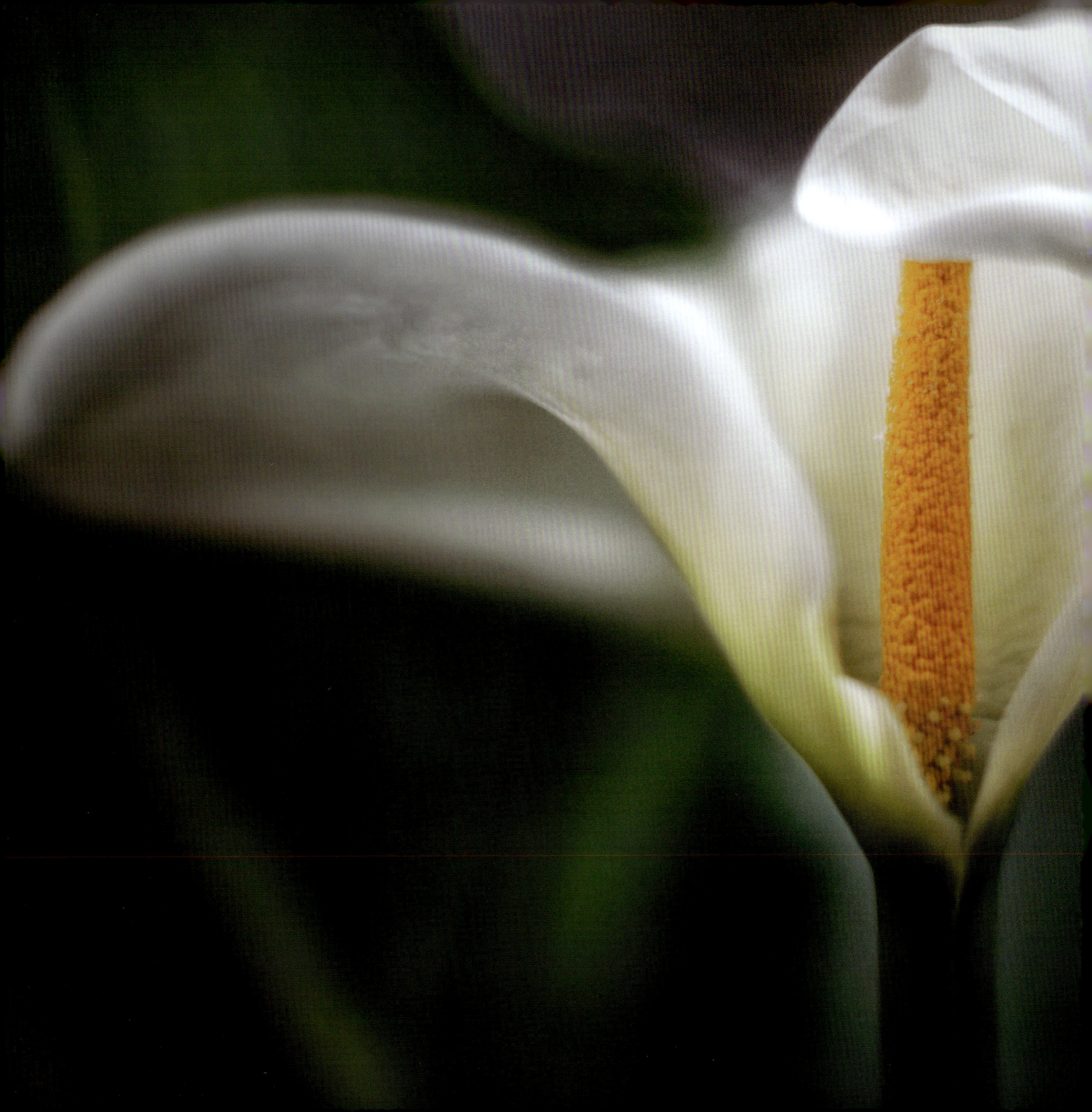

Swerve! Your leaf wraps 'round
tiny flowers—male and female—
blooming on your spadix cupped inside

a spire envied by men
noted by women

How confidently you show yourself!

not even a real lily
toxic to cats and dogs
once a symbol of death

but that time is past
if not for cats and dogs

Greedy, sway is not enough for you!
Having no scent, you wear perfumed colors.

Is that what poison does?
Double down on enticement?

No matter. We are seduced
but will not eat you.

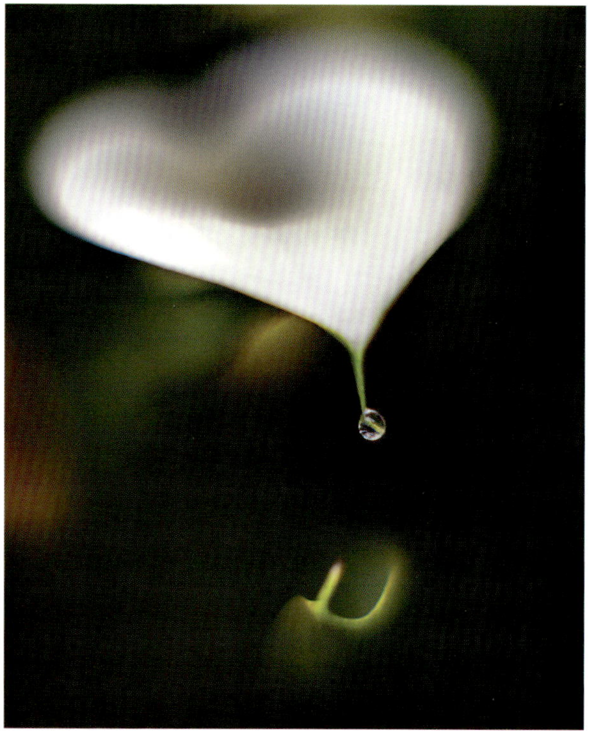

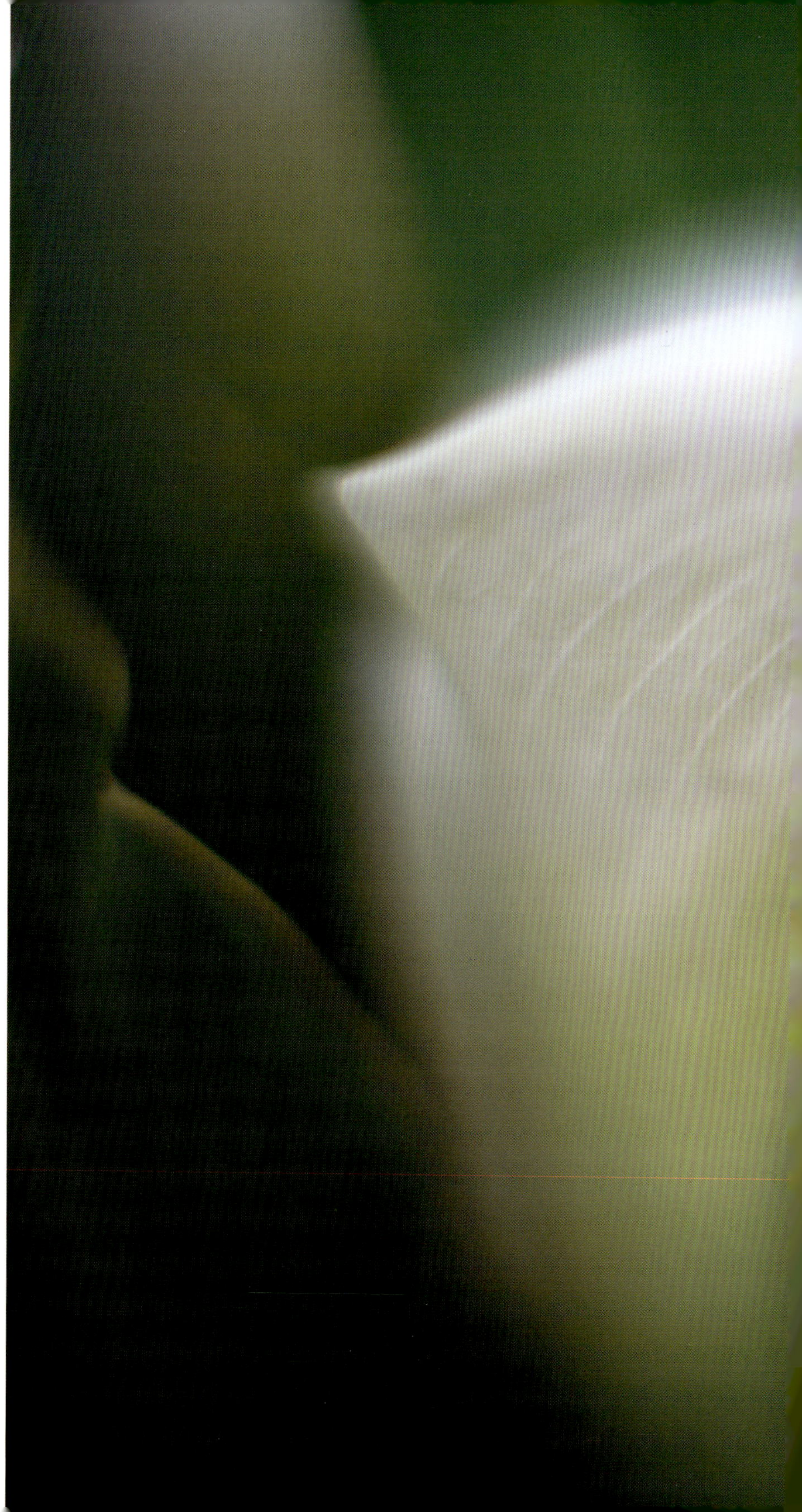

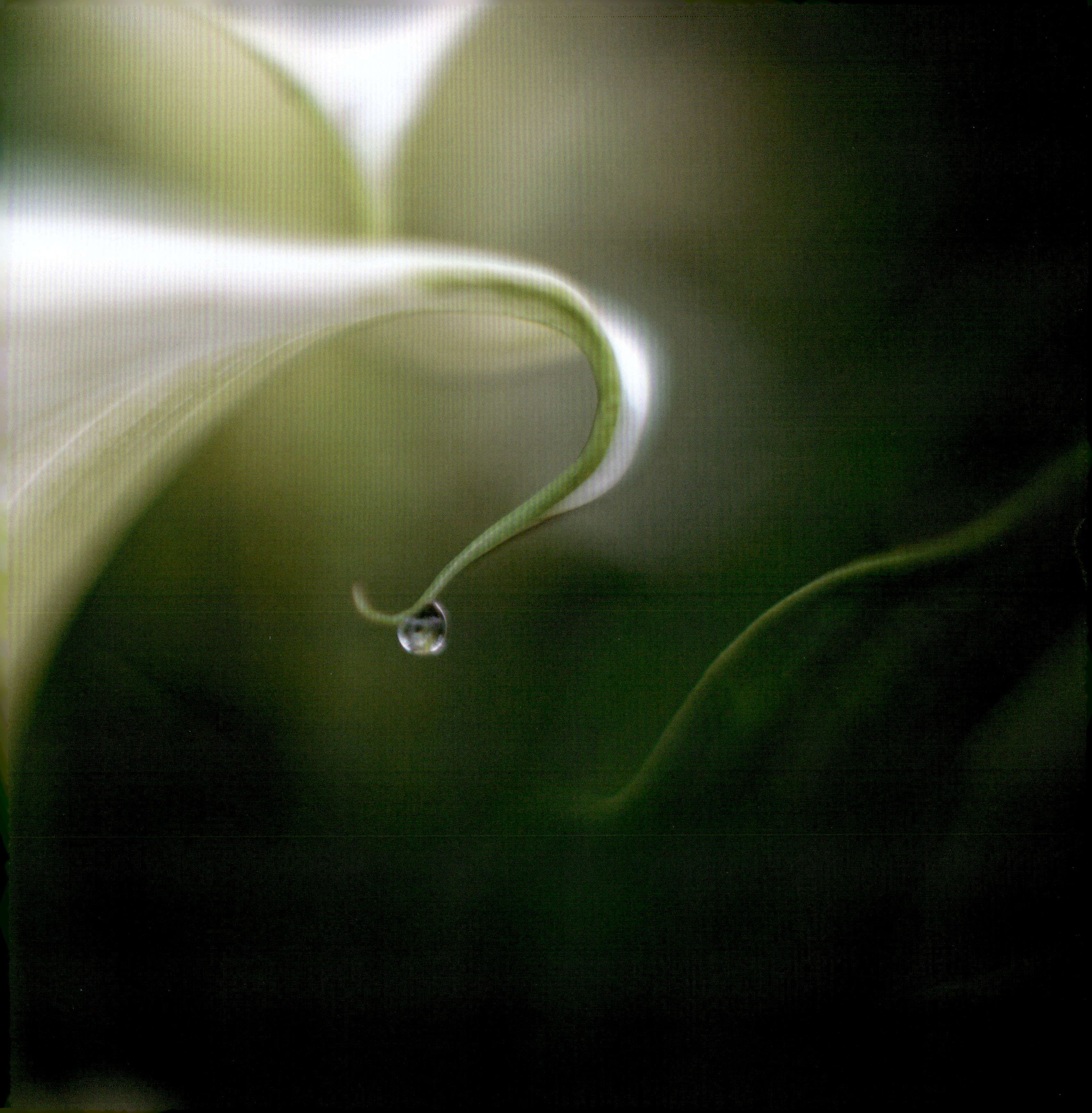

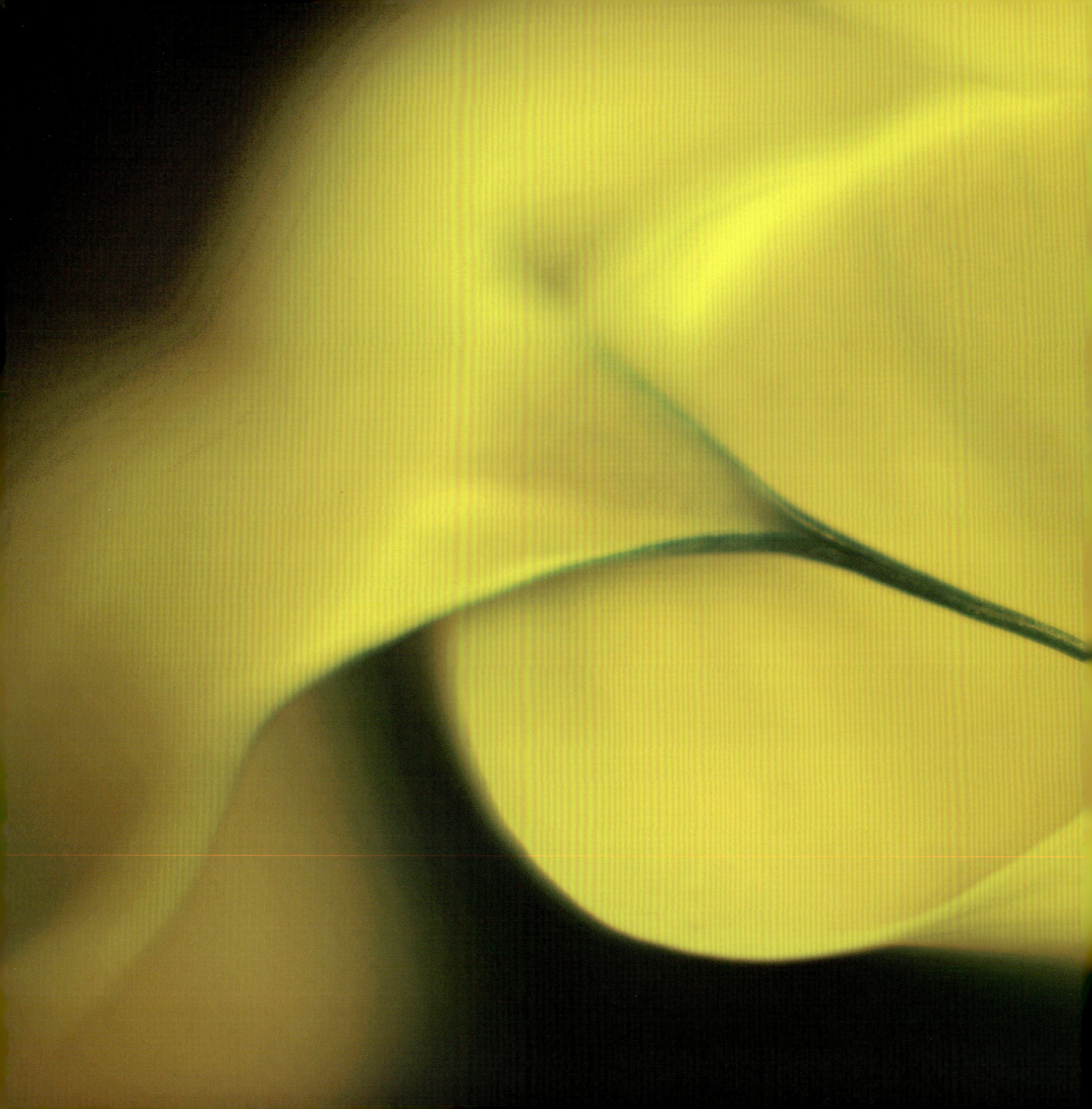

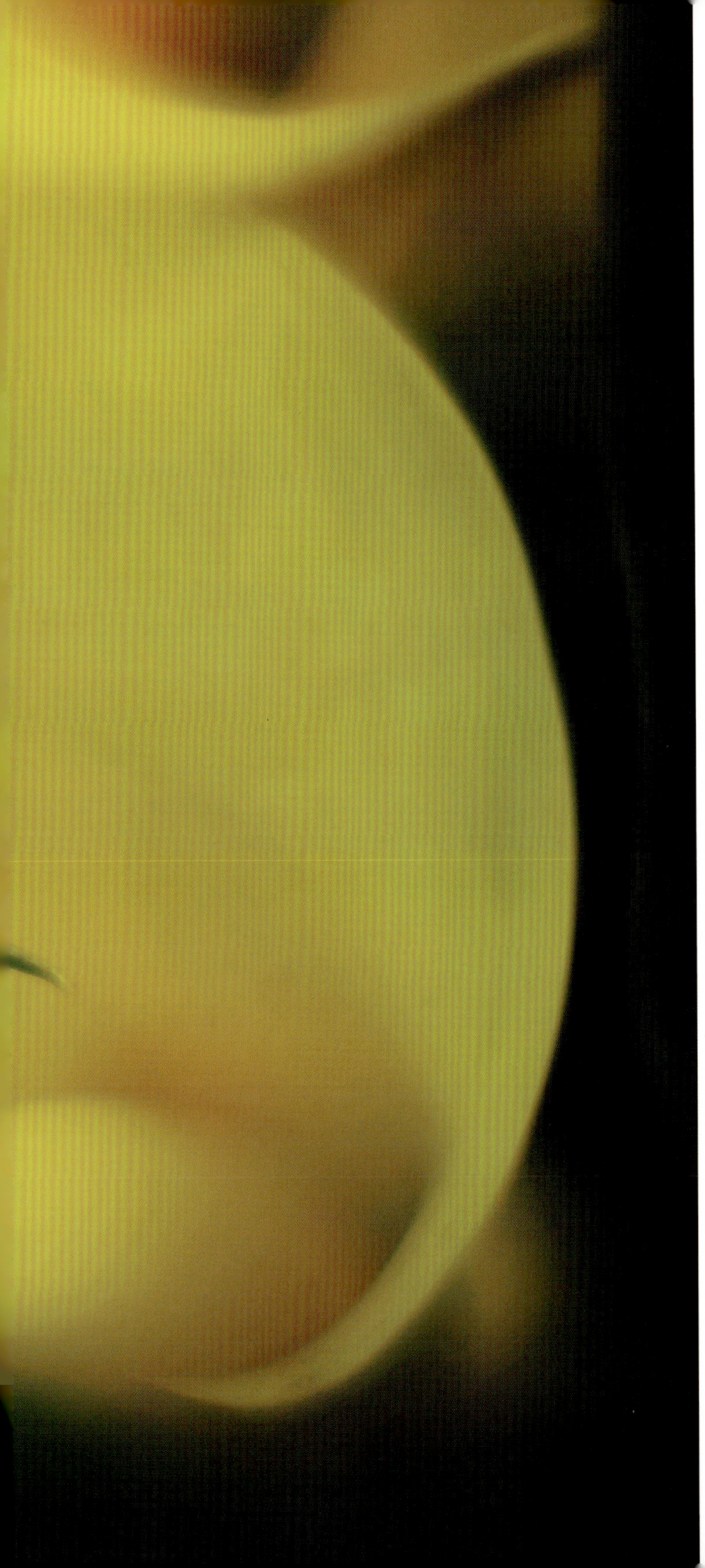

The difference between pierce
and caress is known best
by the receiver, not the giver.

Allow for mistakes,
misjudgment of distance,
and the way the wind blows
at any given moment.

But only if you feel so inclined.

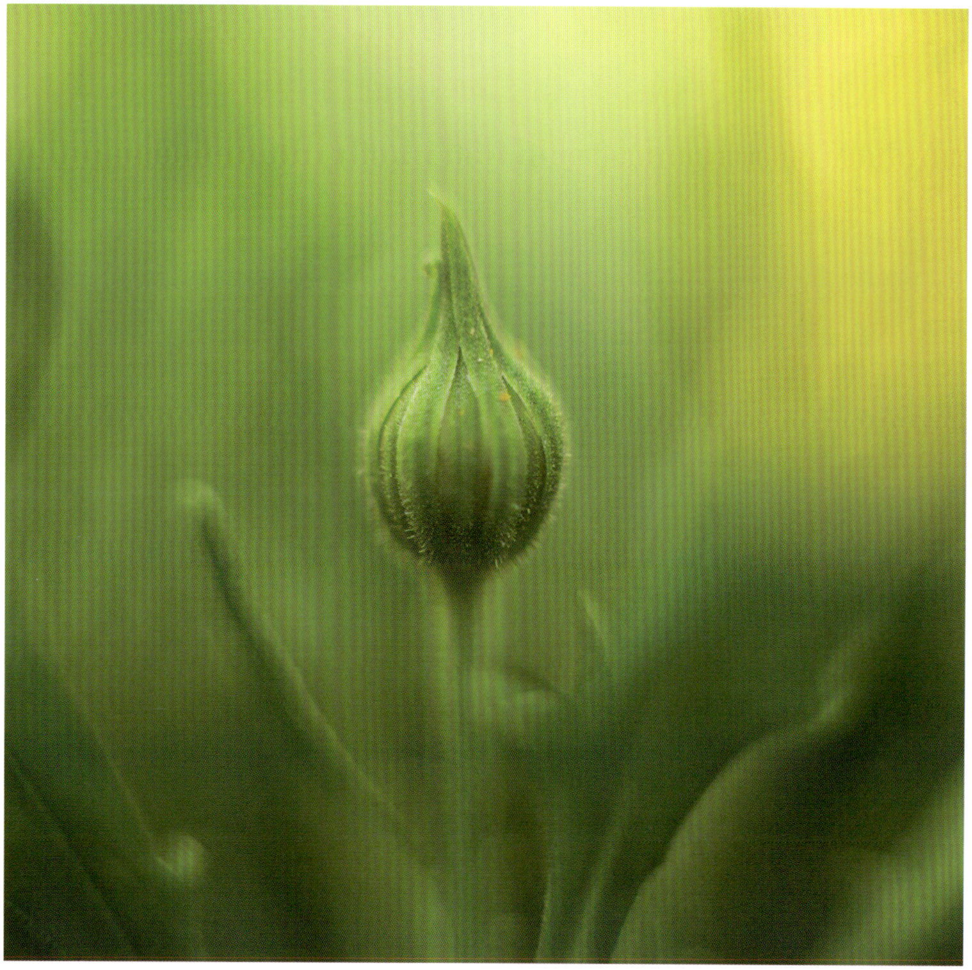

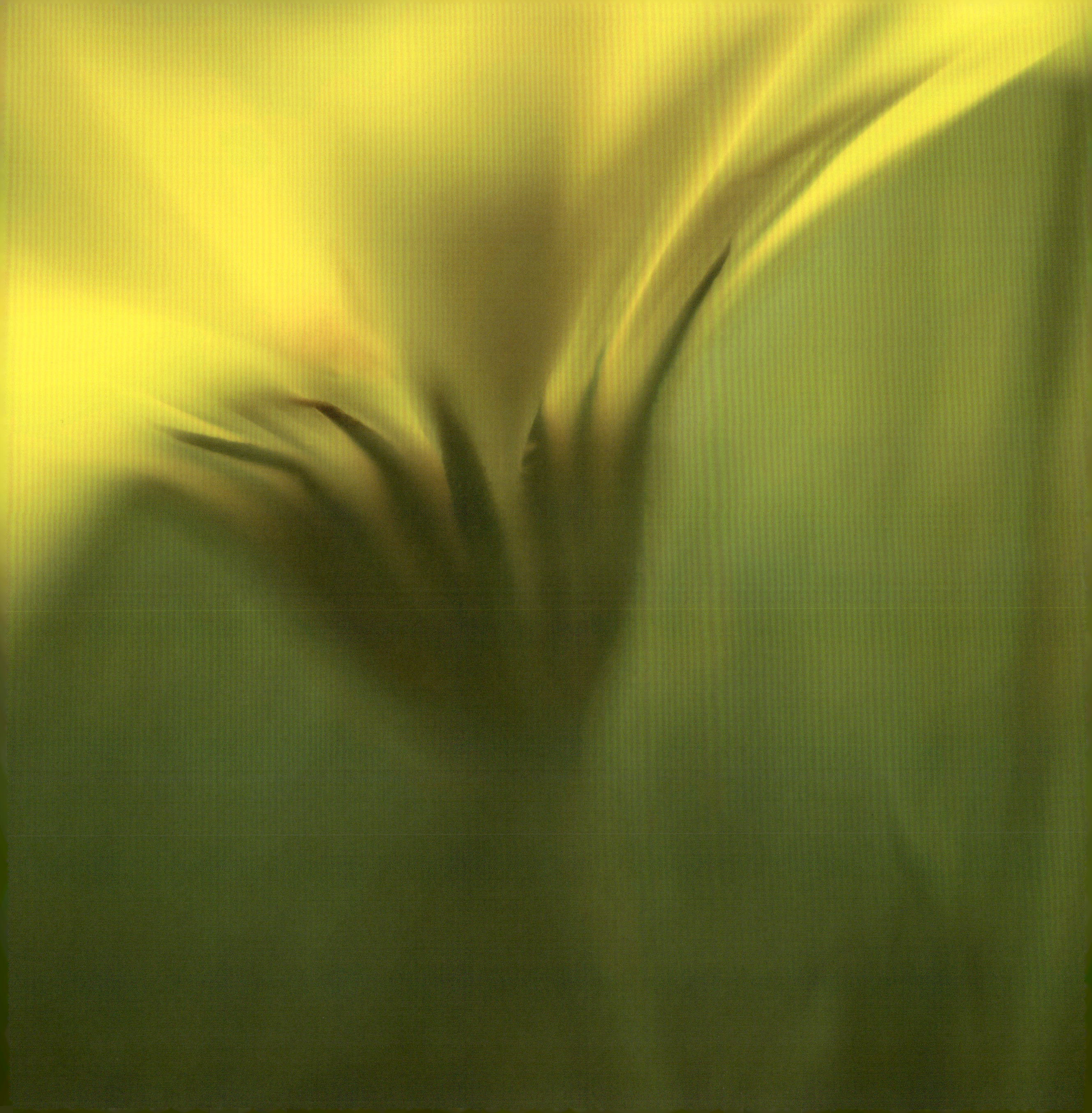

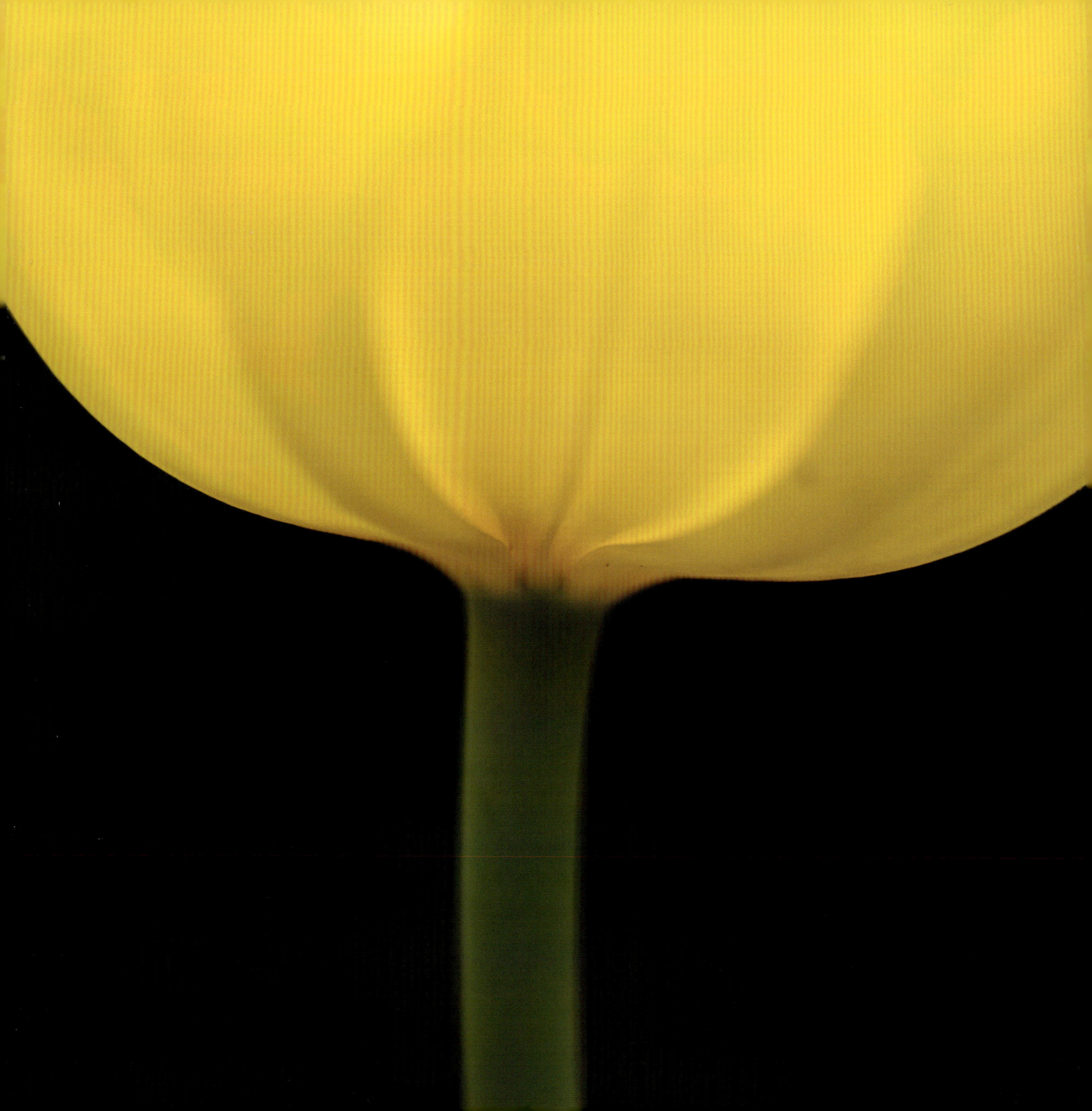

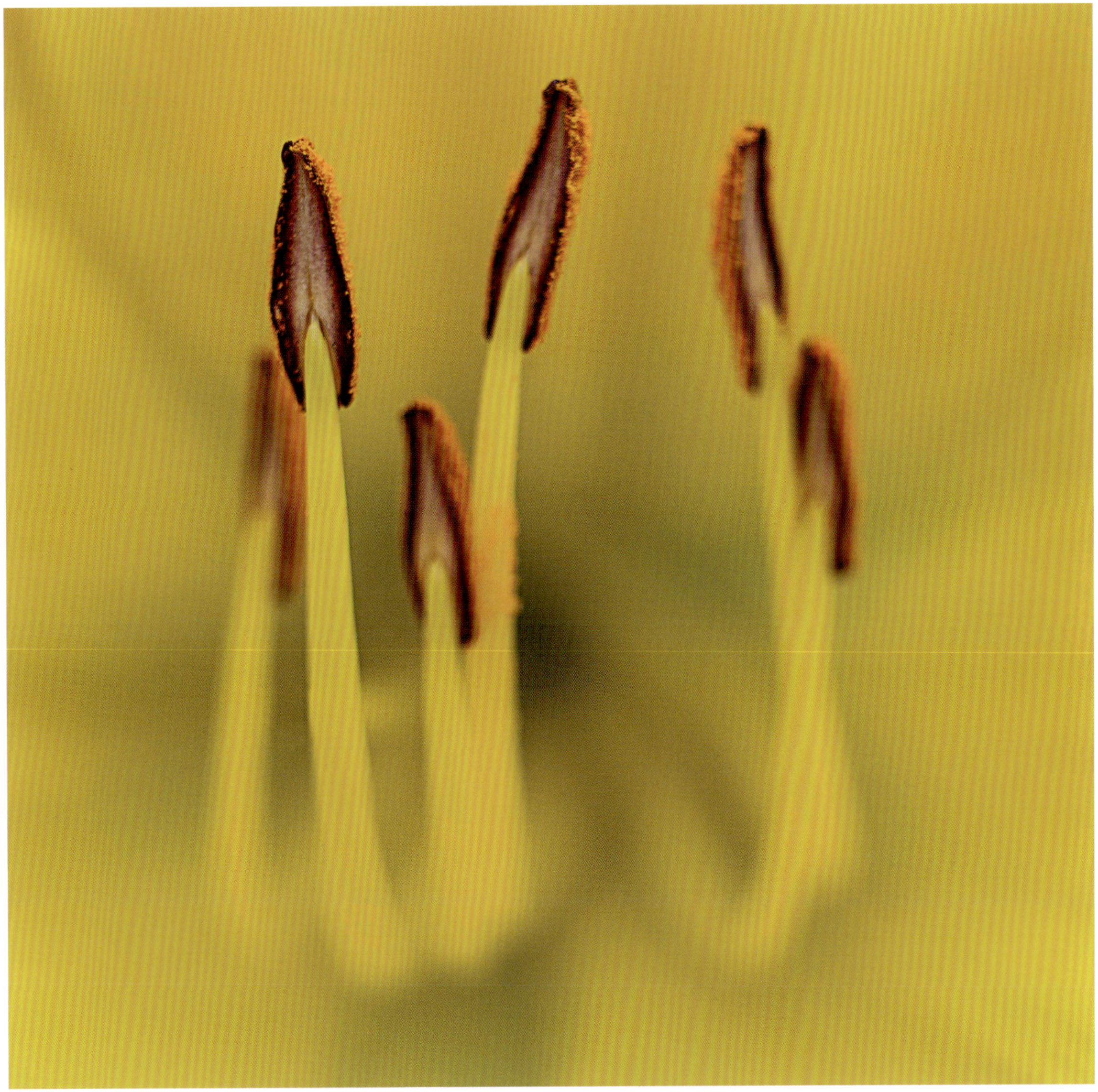

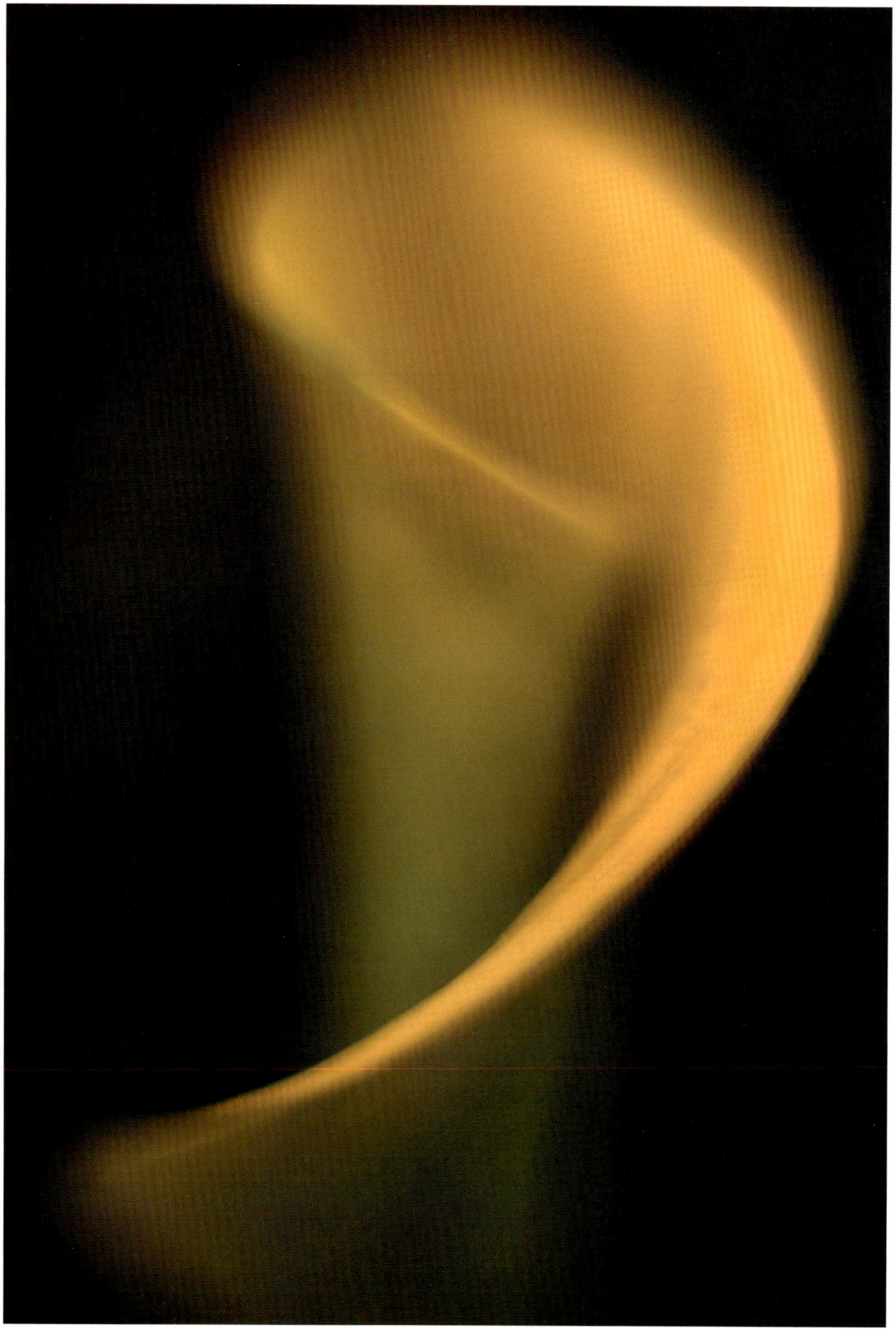

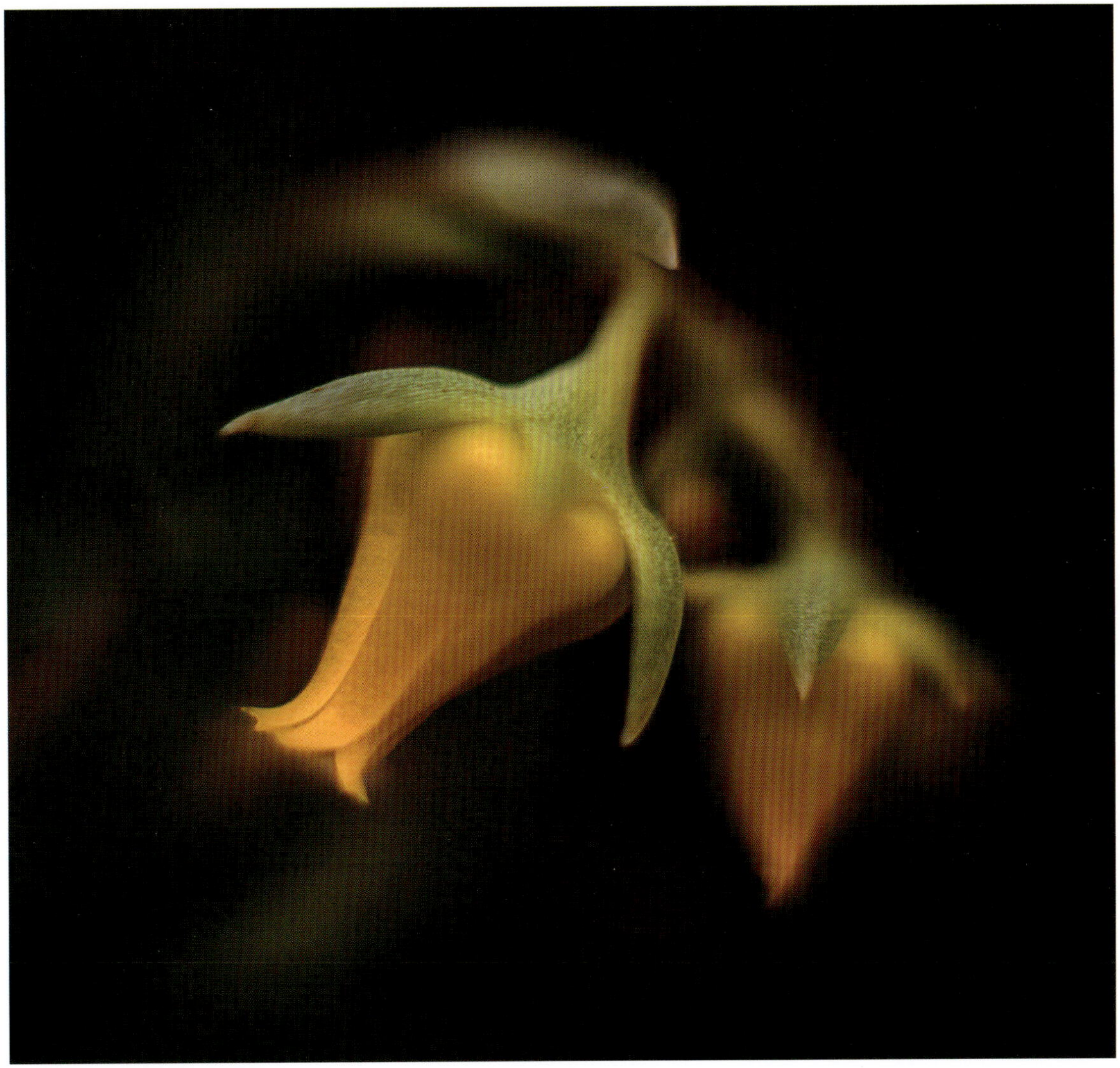

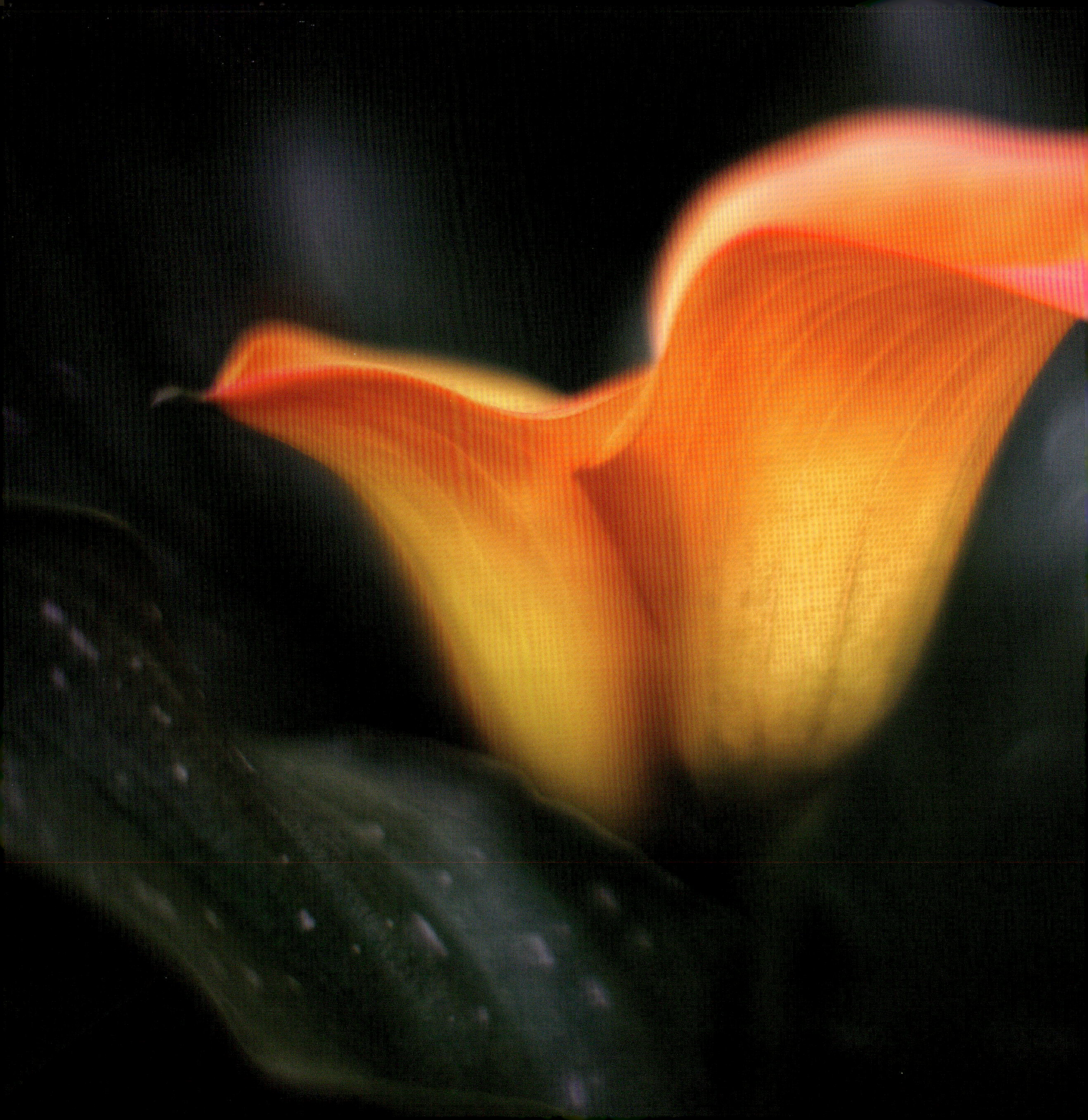

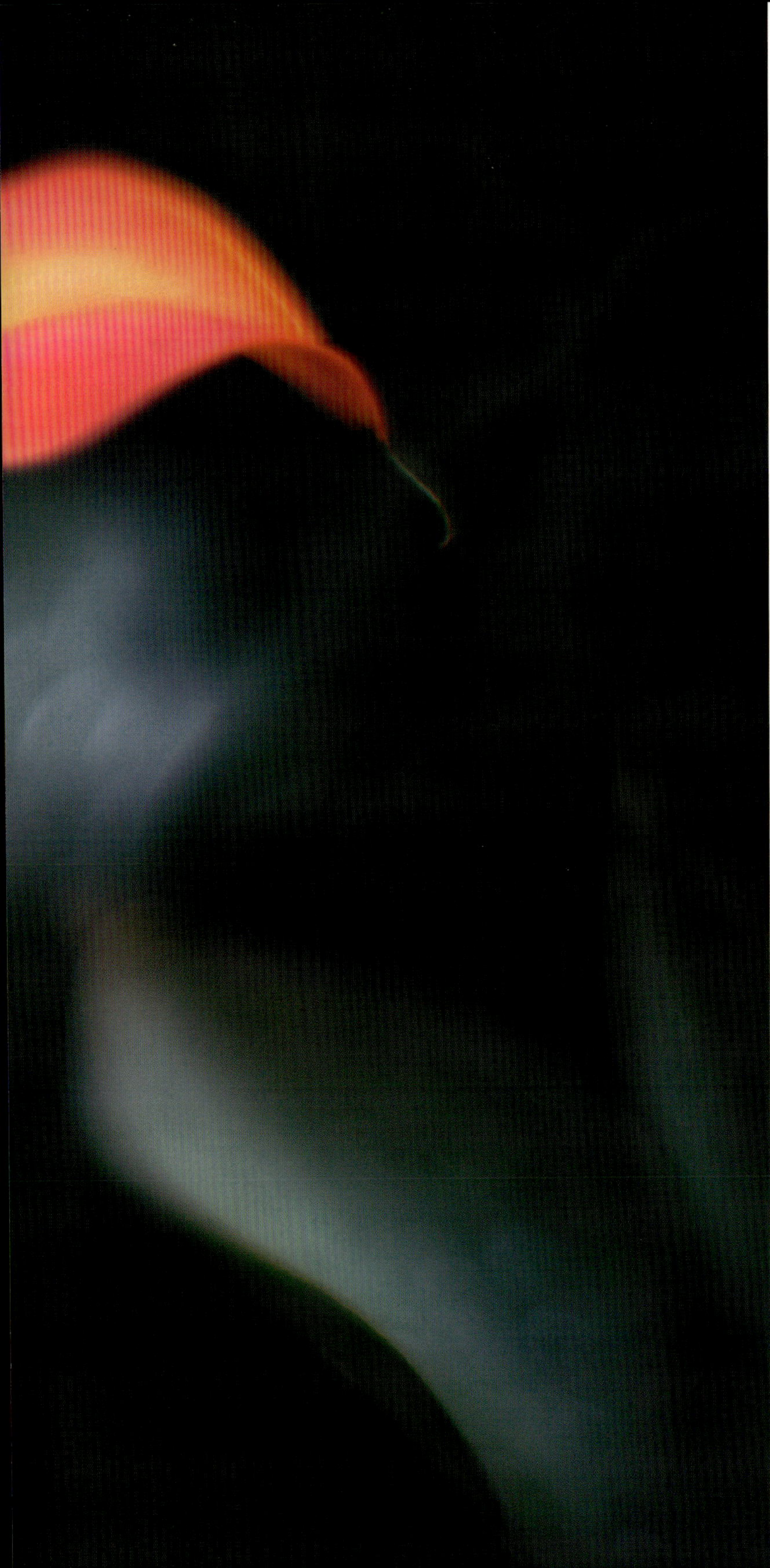

The season of sweetness and renewal
is short—
    sun
    rain
    dew
    breeze
    penetration by winged creatures
    yielding
    fading

So much to do just in being a flower.

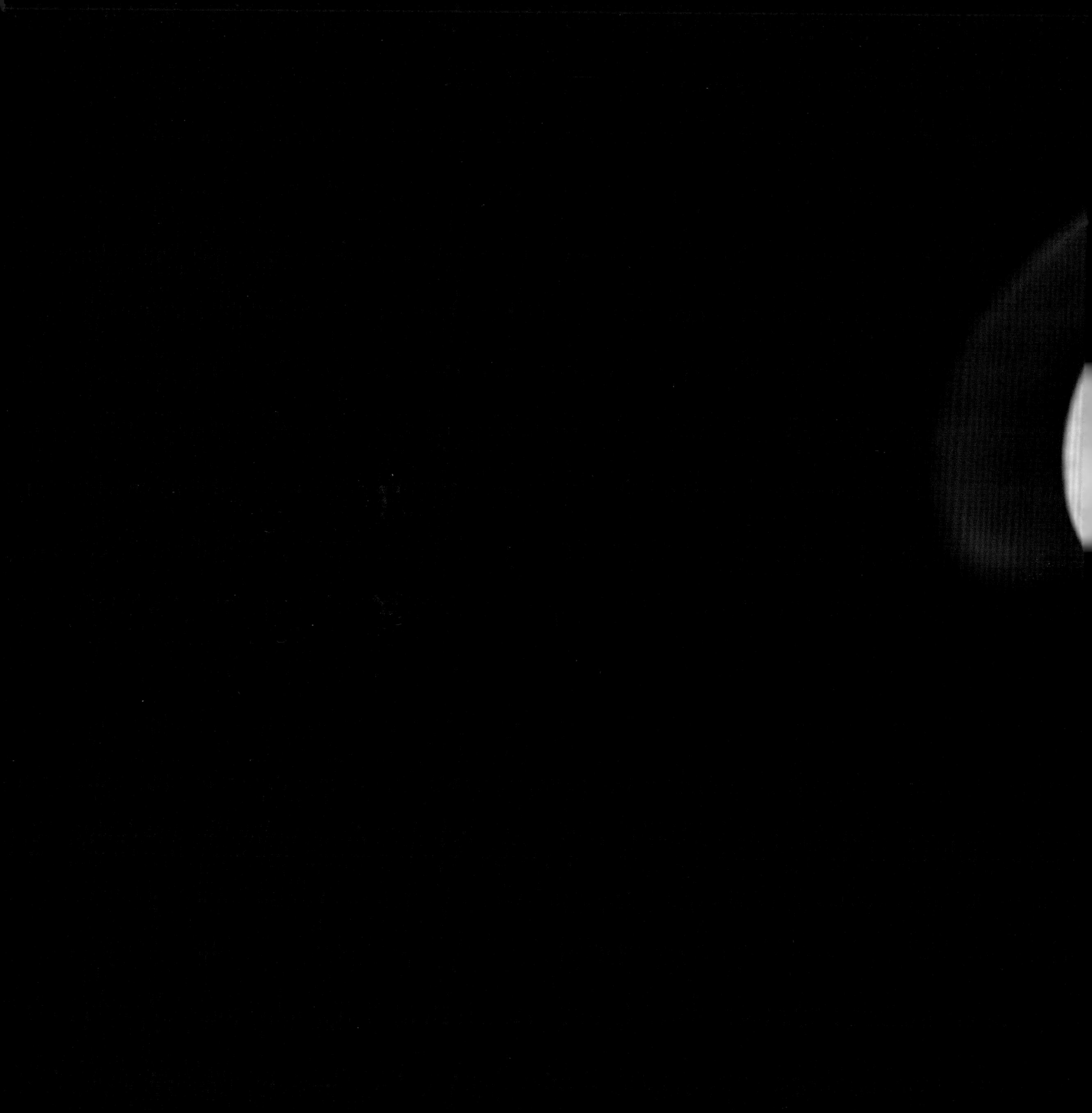

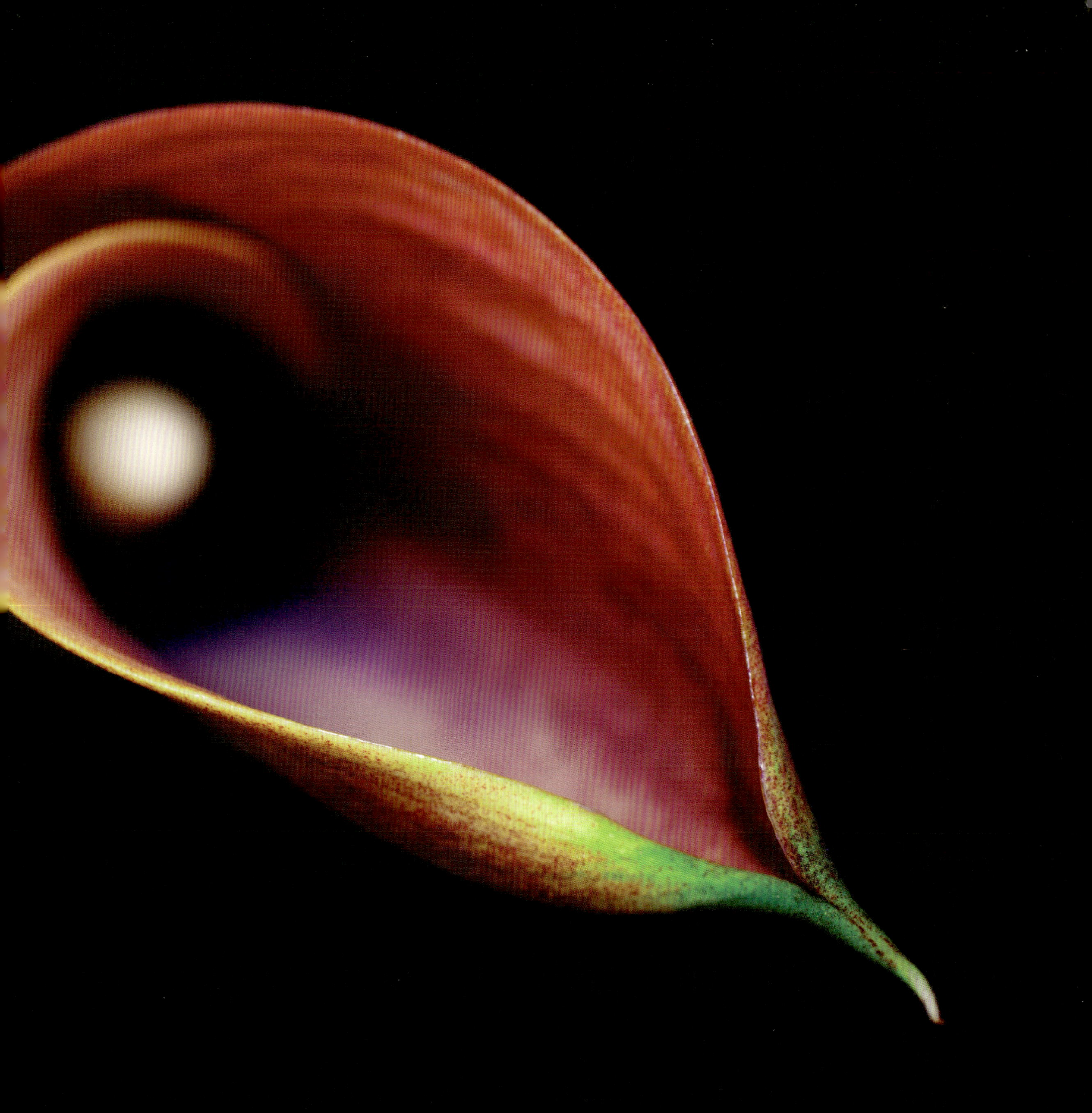

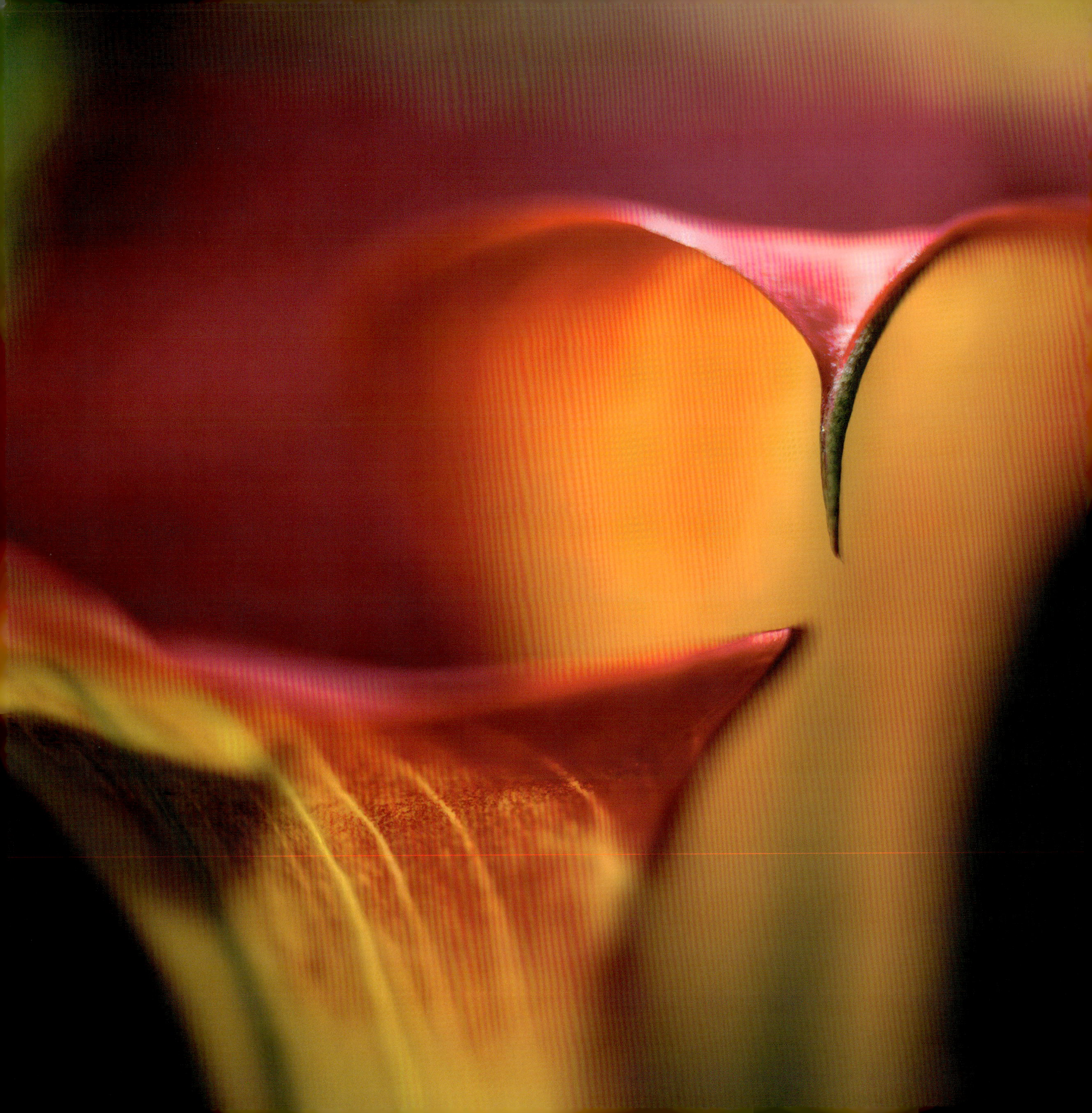

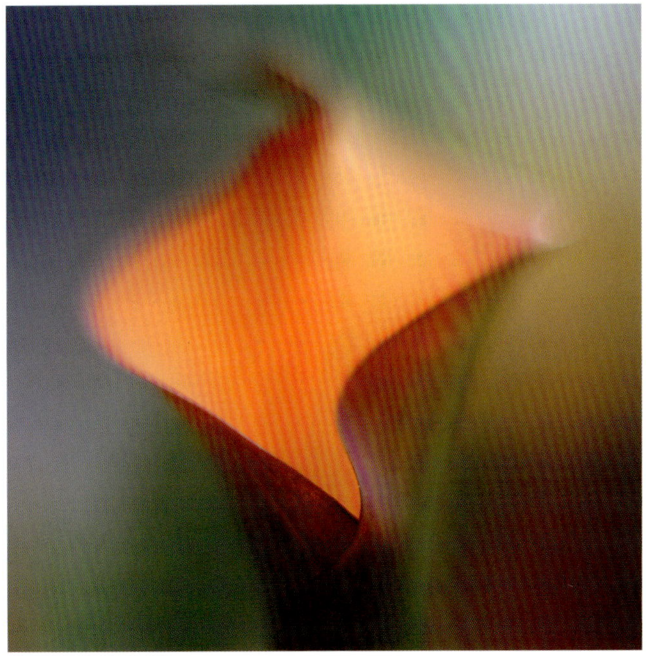

If orange be the color of madness,
be mad

with a hint of carmen
and blush of rose.

Ablaze!

with who you once were
and long to be again

pulsating passion—
orange with a drop of blood.

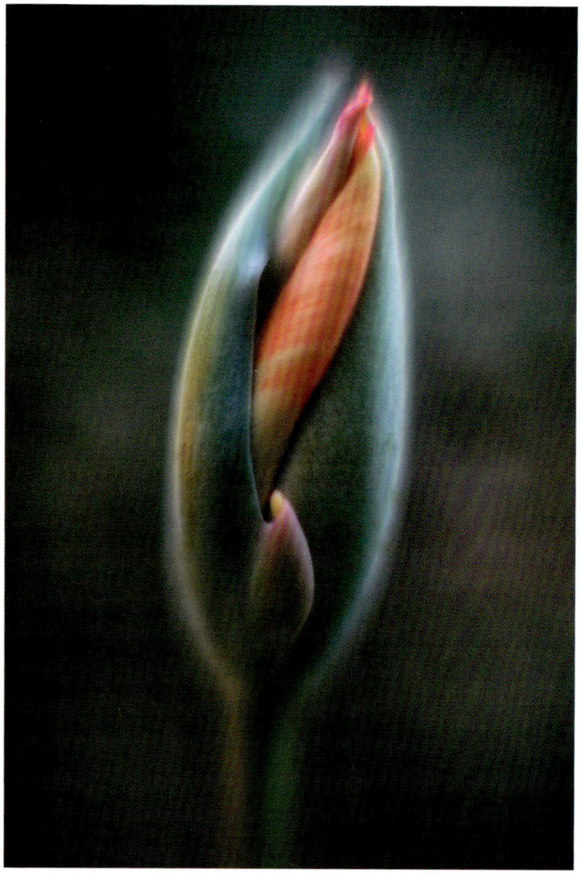

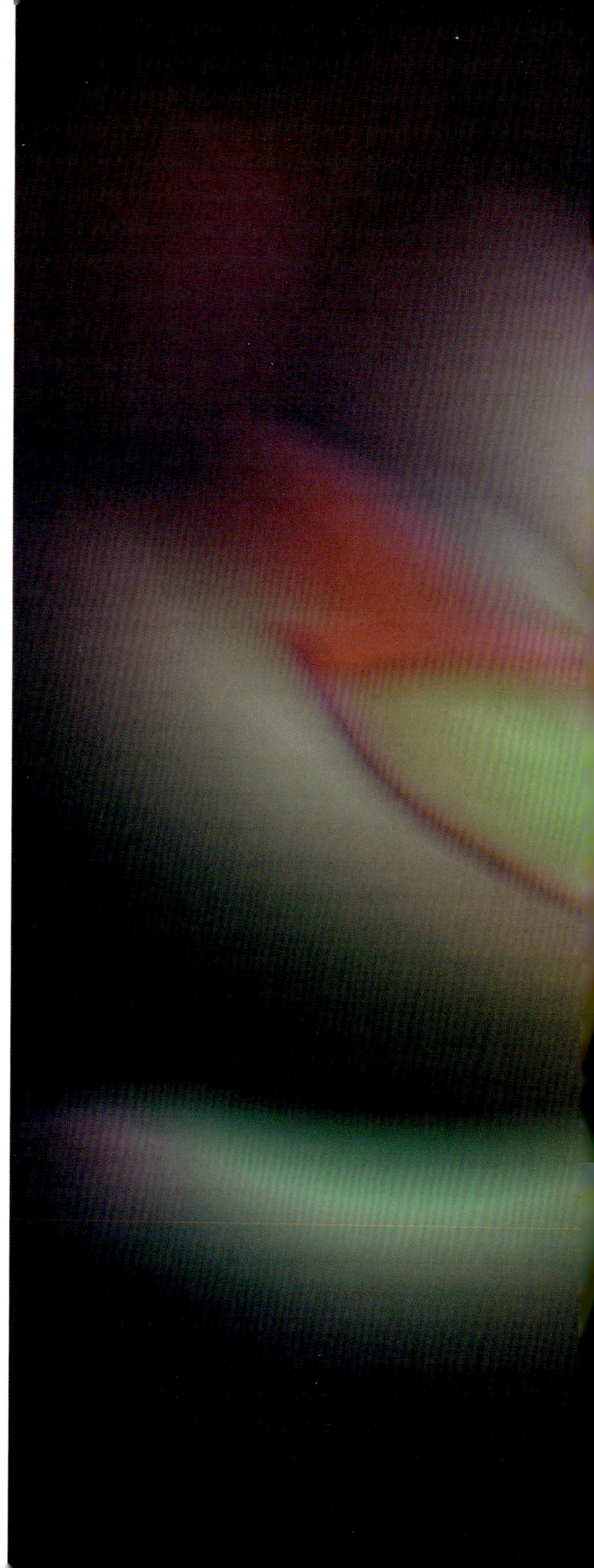

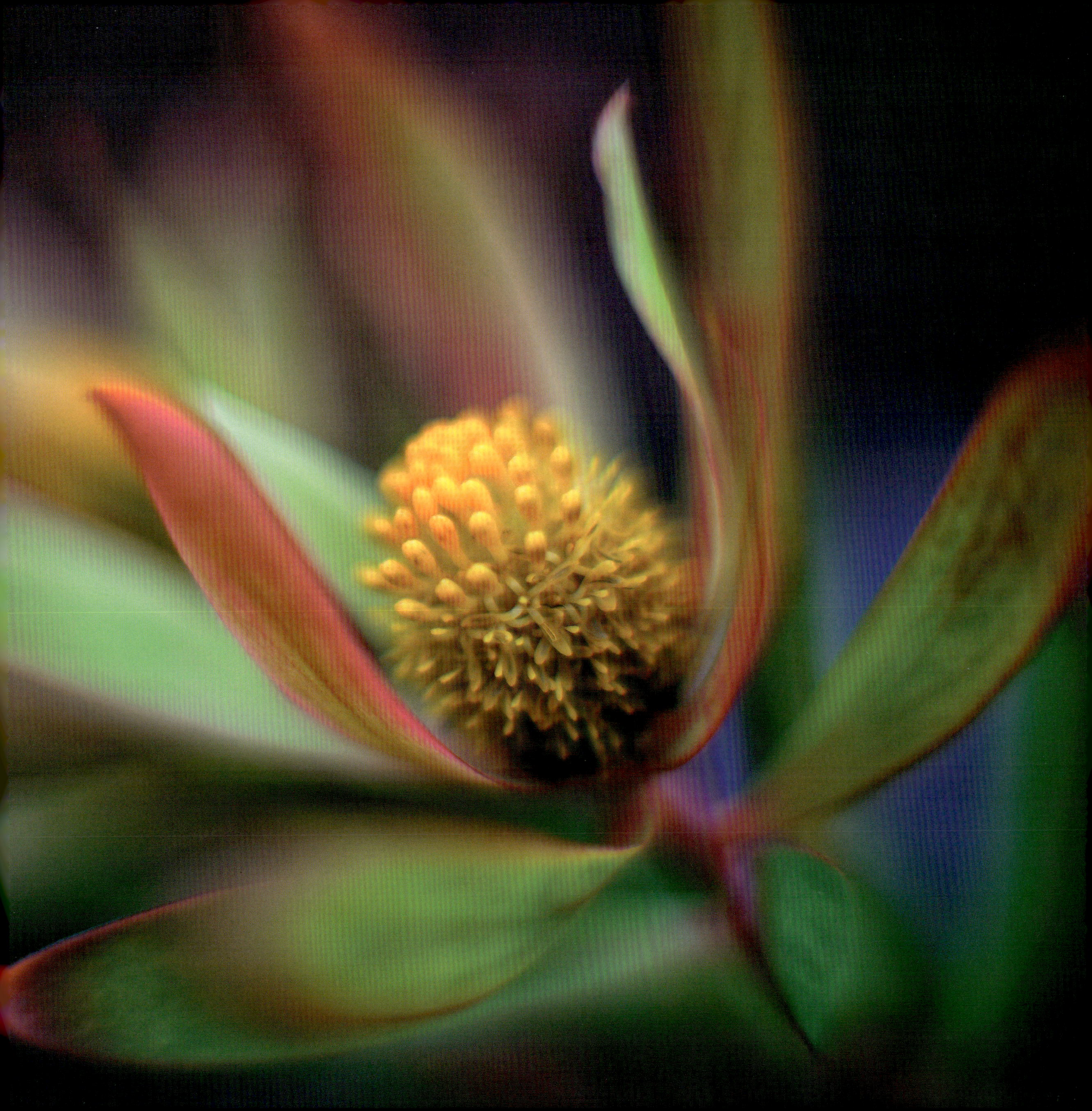

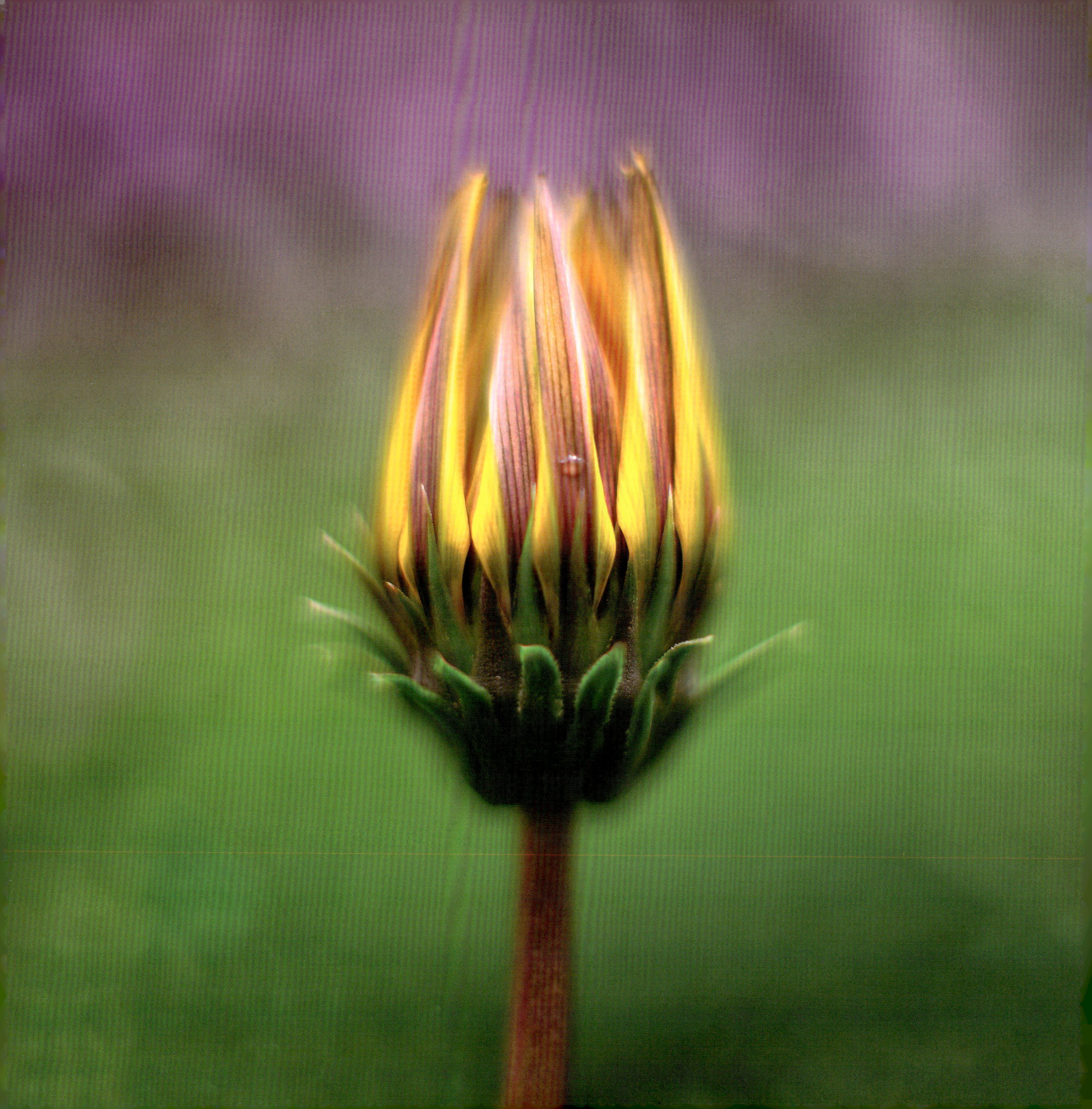

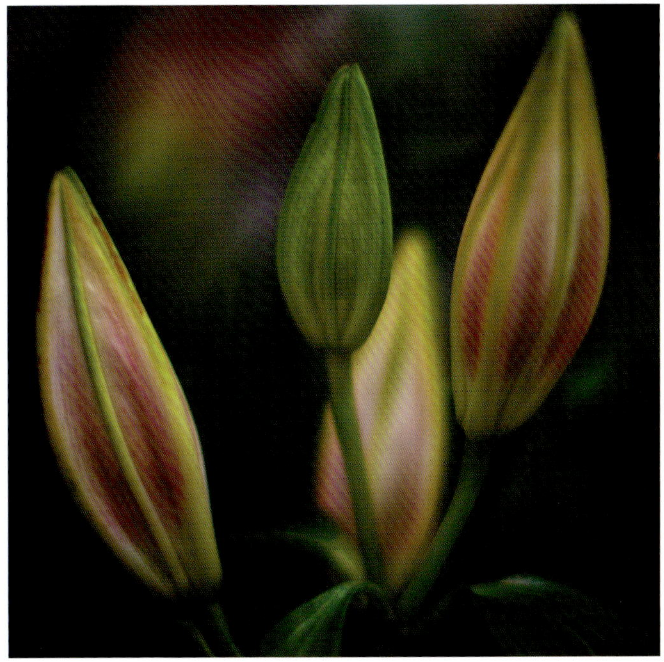

Don't cut me.

I am here for birds, butterflies,
dragonflies, damselflies,
and so many bees
you can never count them.

Their thirst and ravages
are sweeter than your castration
and infertile triflings.

The common daisy *Bellis perennis* does not envy the *Paphiopedilum* orchid—
never thought "that showoff thinks it's better than I am."

The *Verbene bonariensis* does not compare itself to the bearded iris—
jealousy never disturbs its peace.

They share rain, sun, and wind equally.

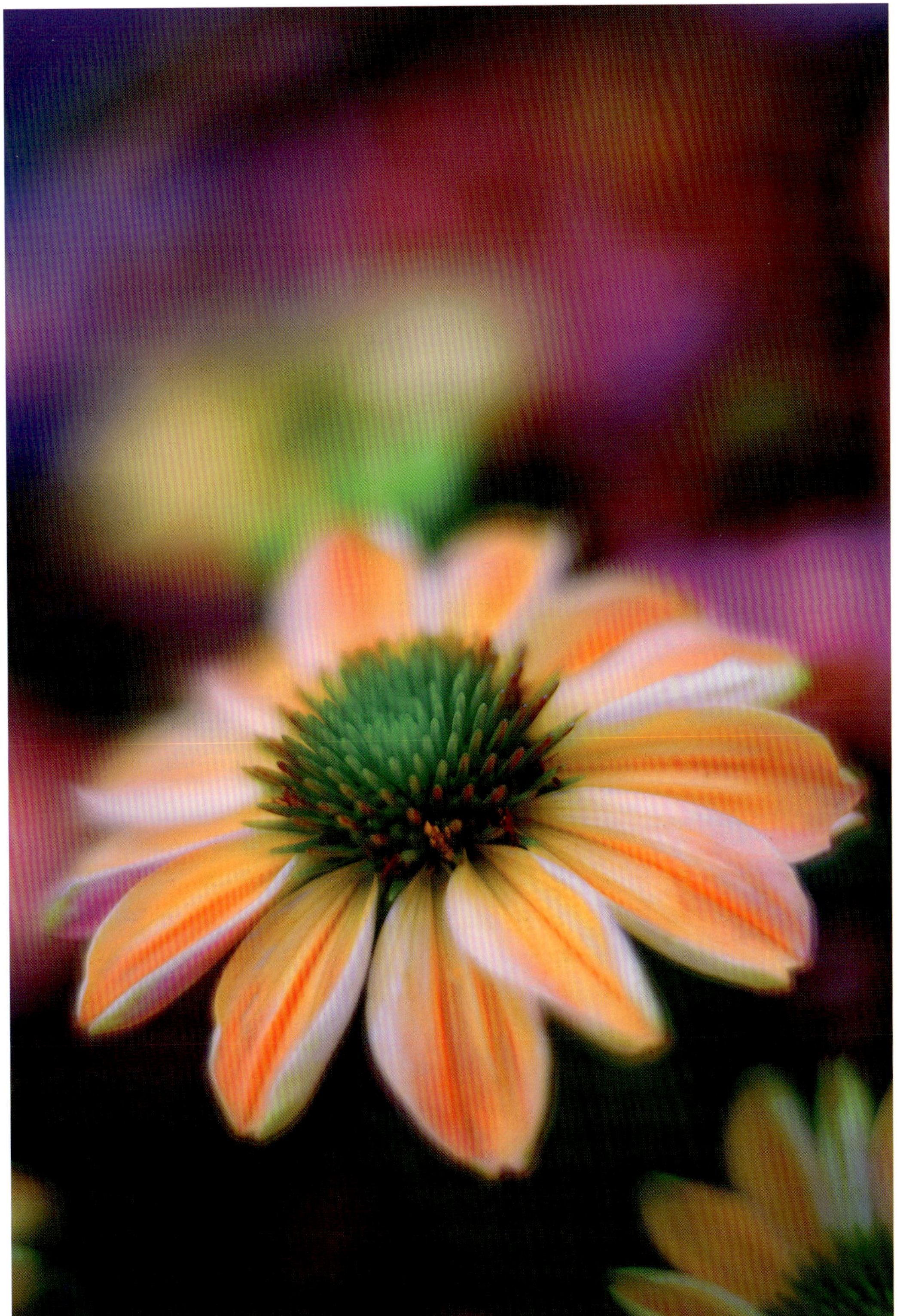

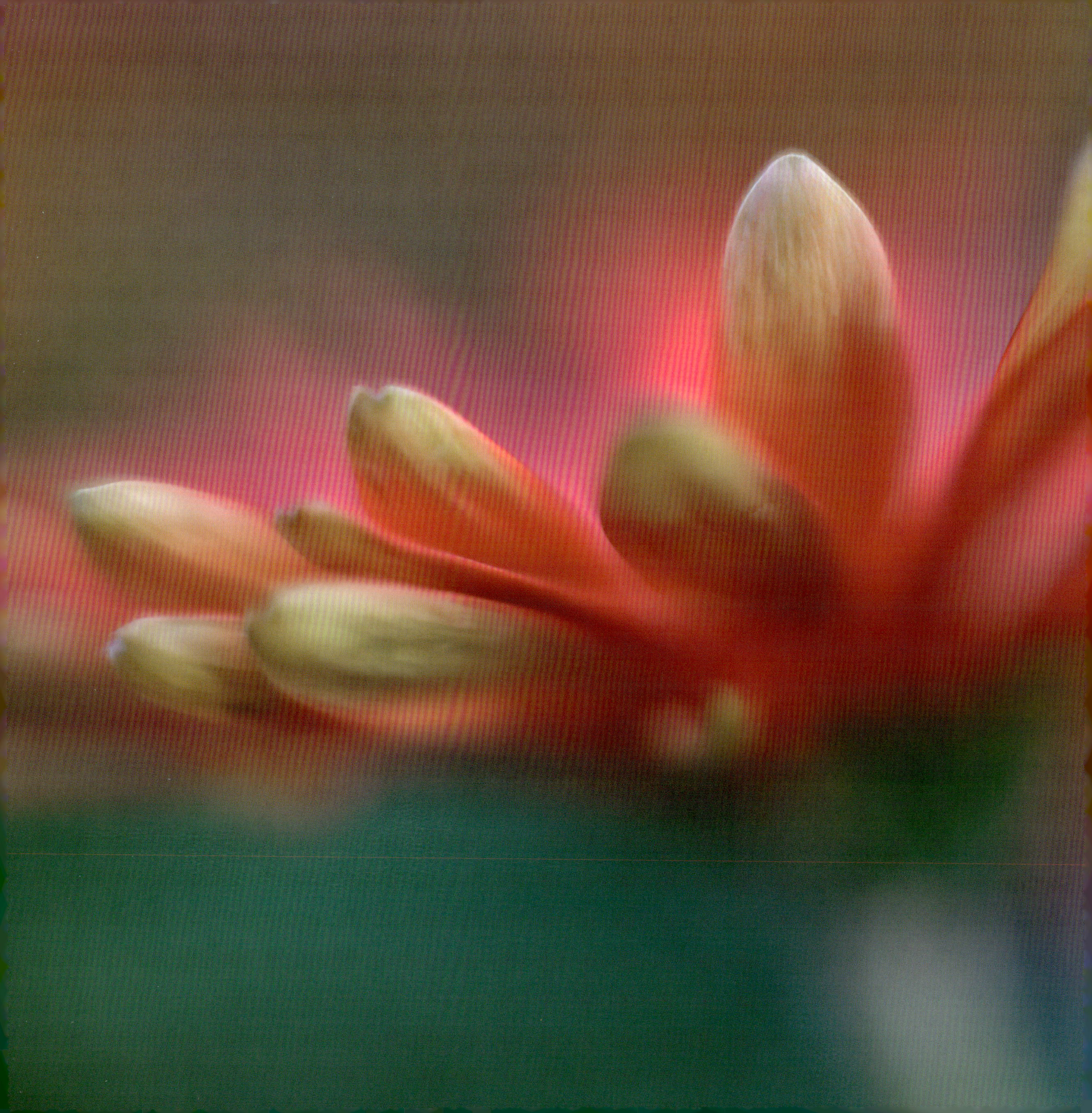

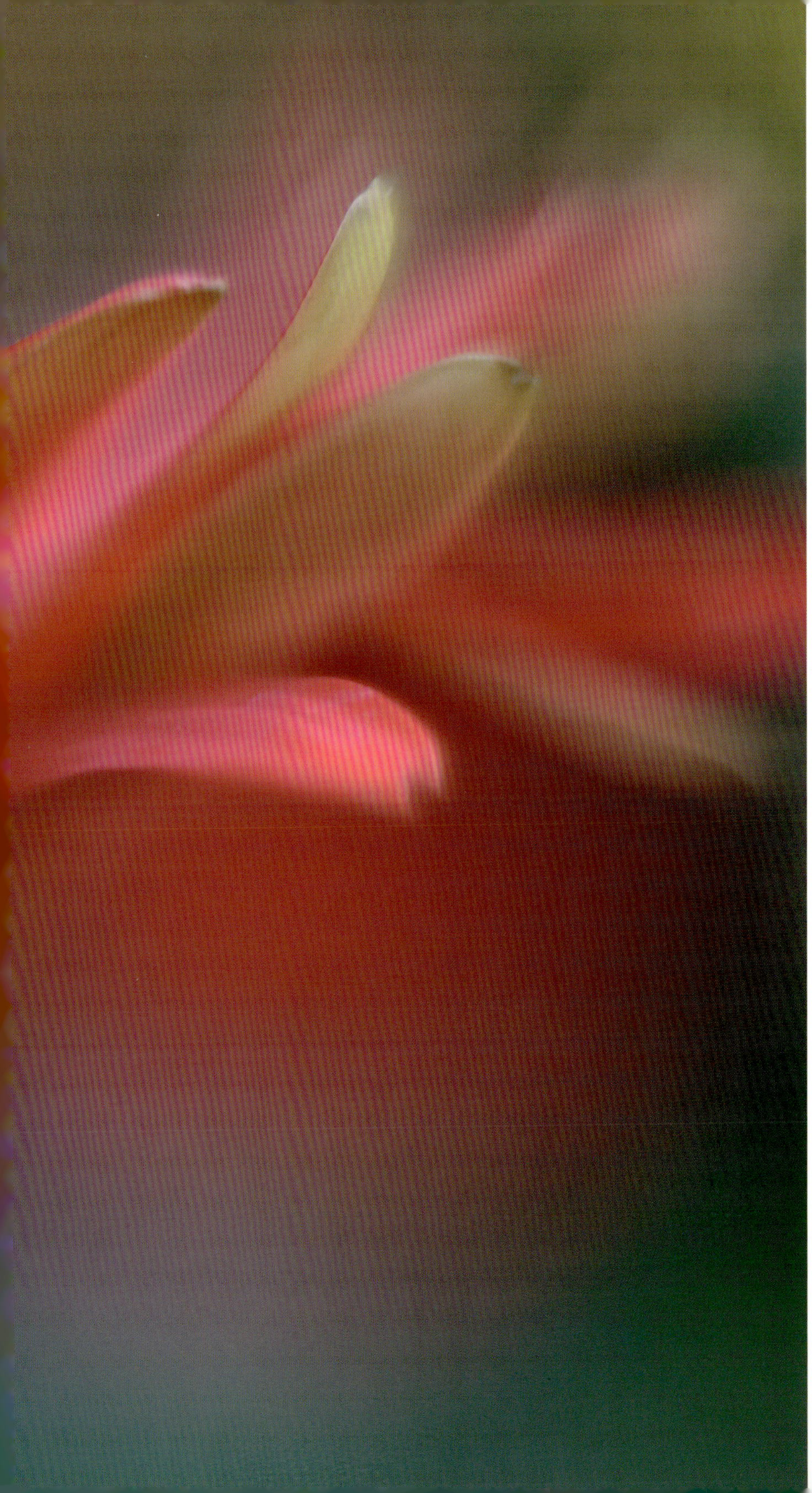

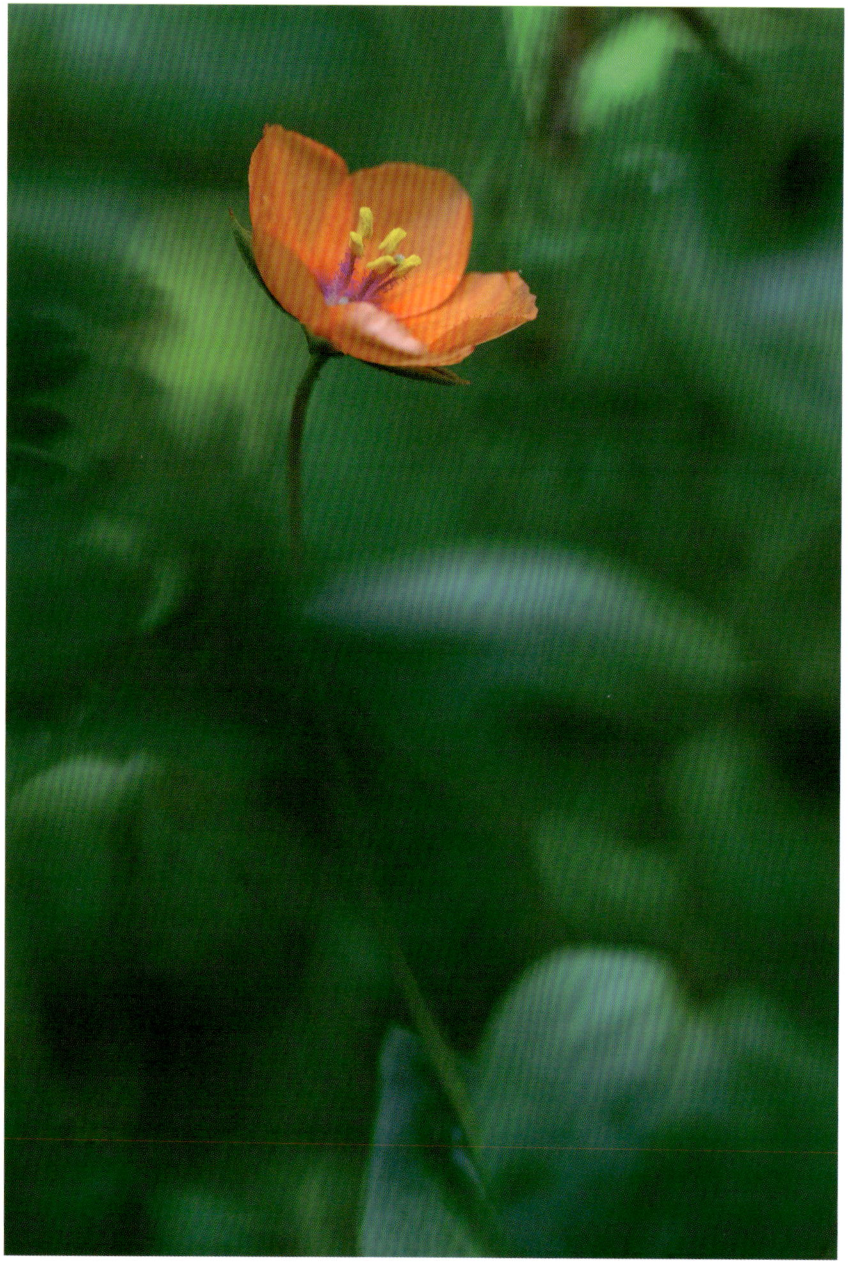

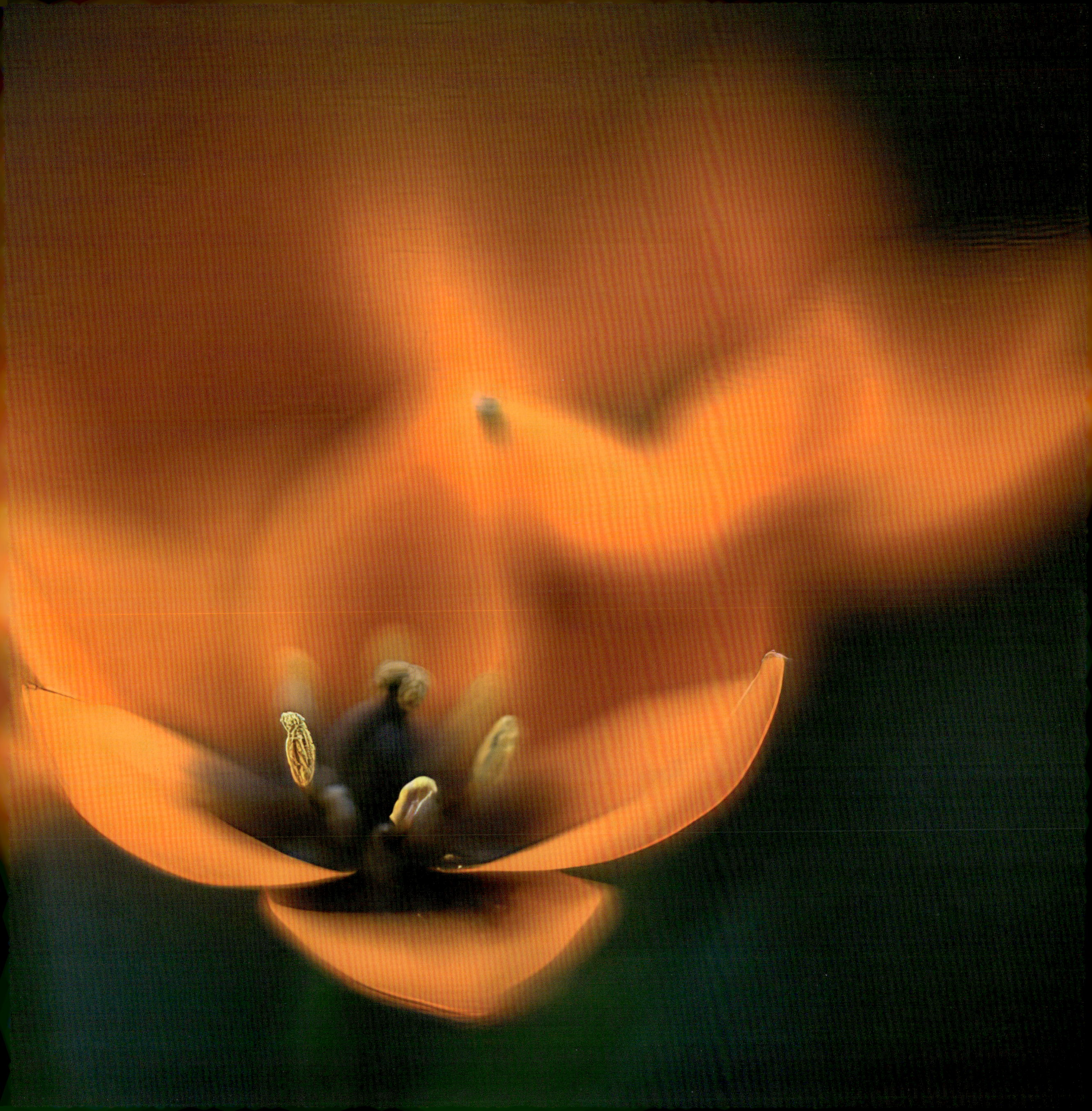

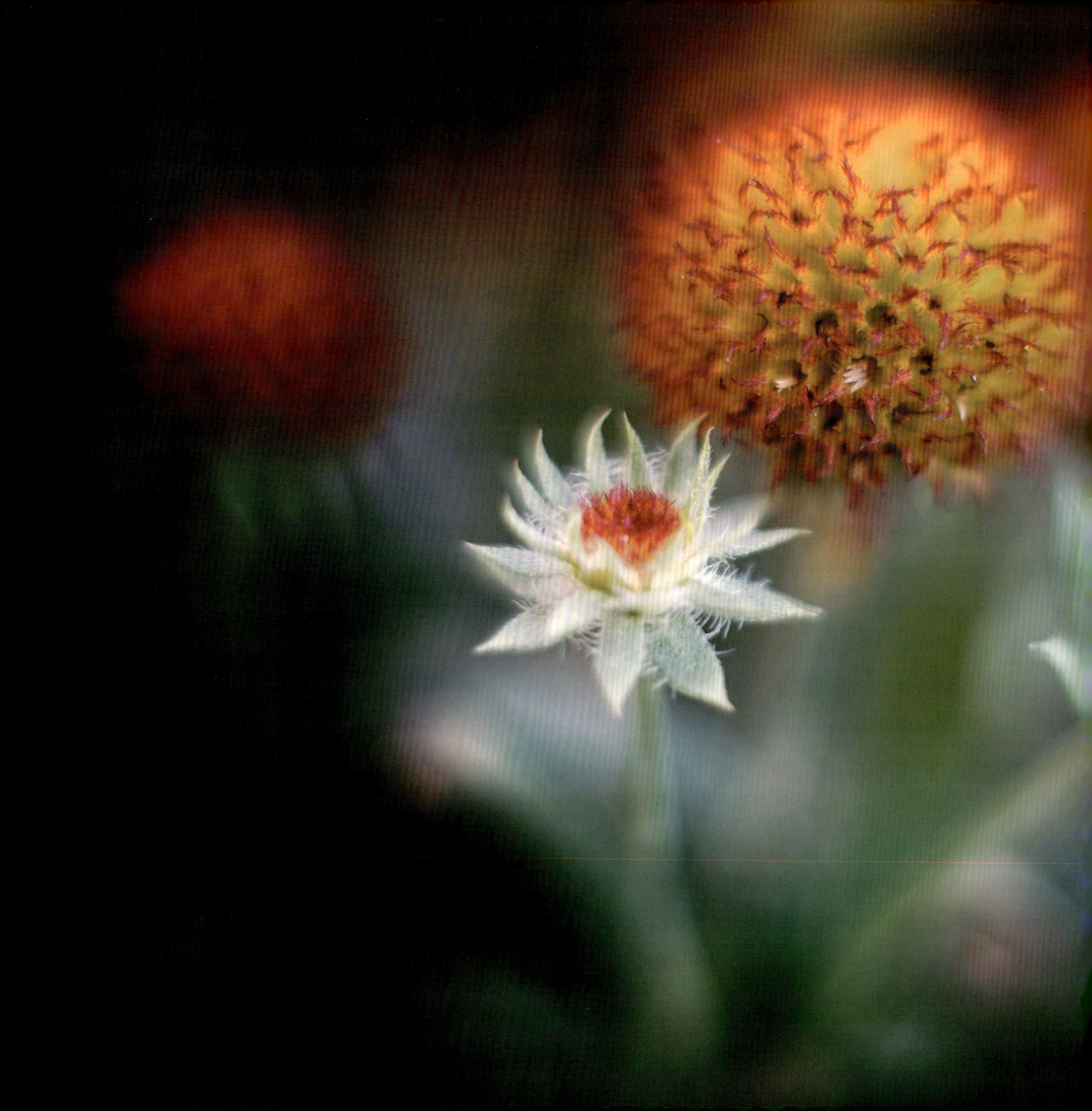

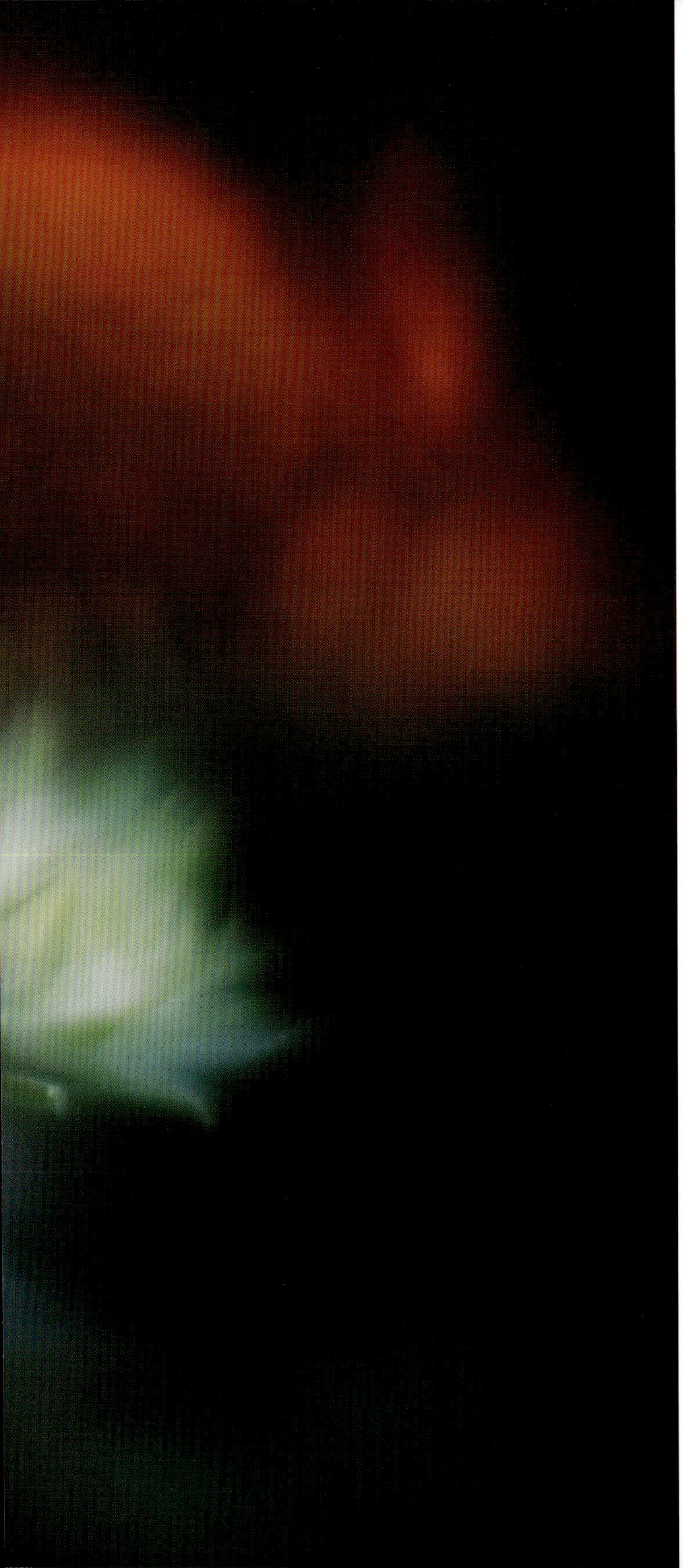

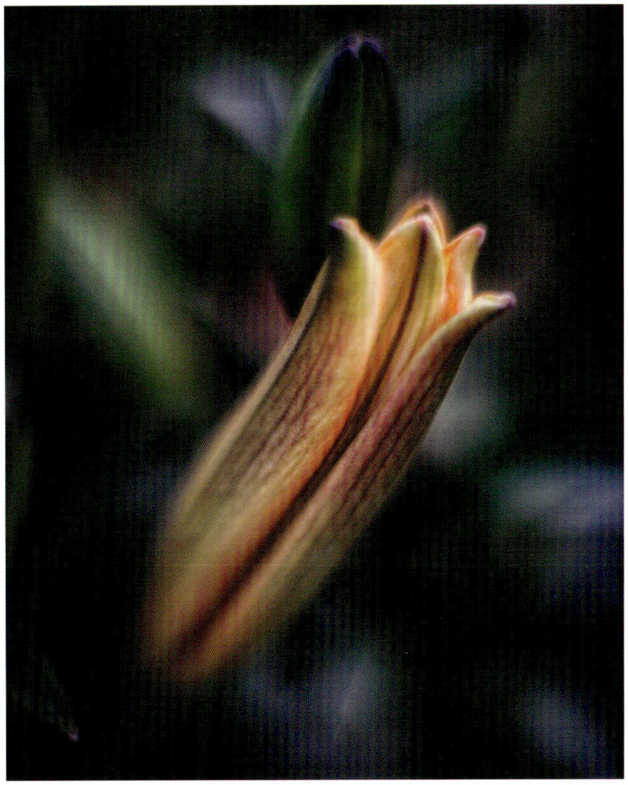

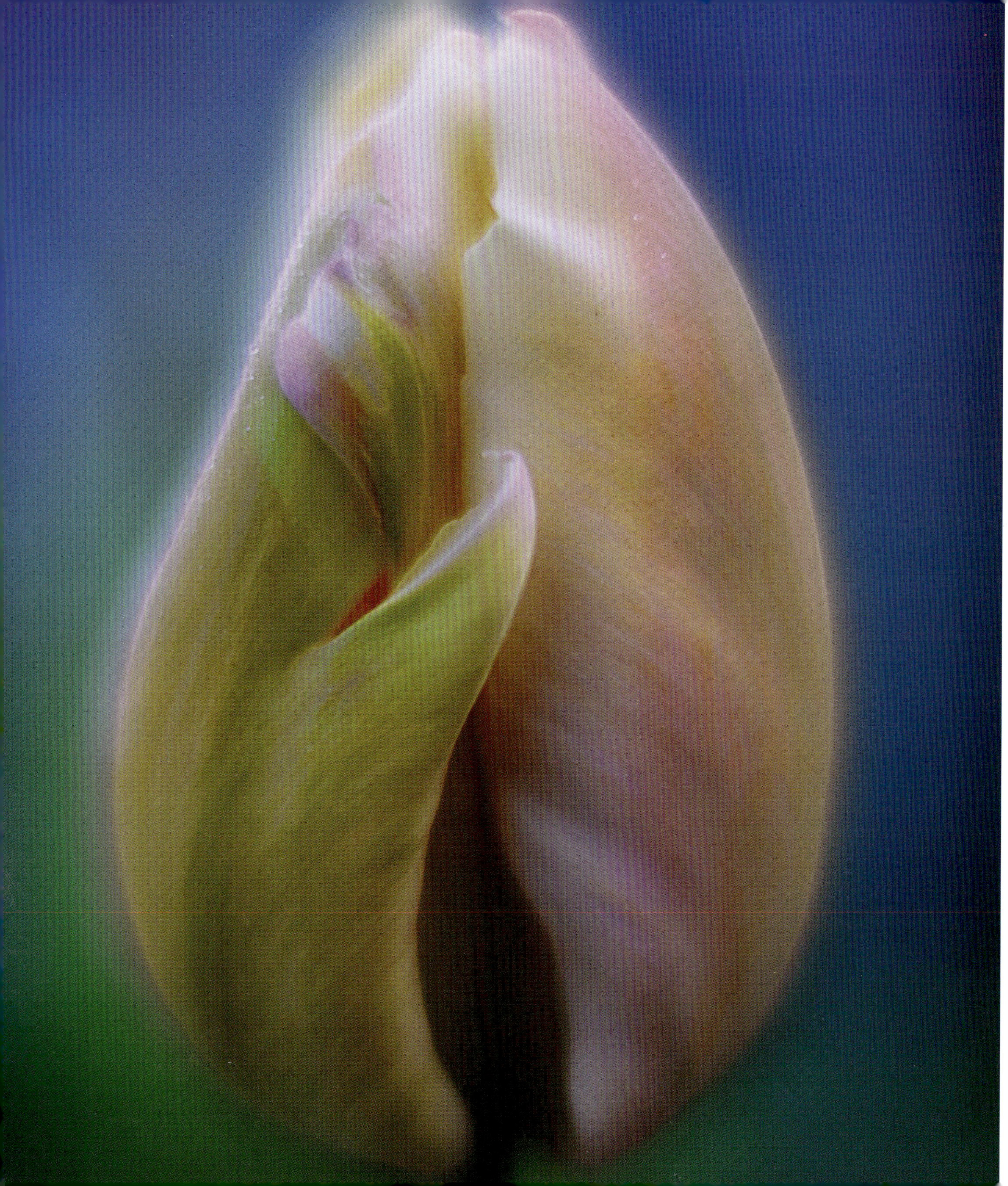

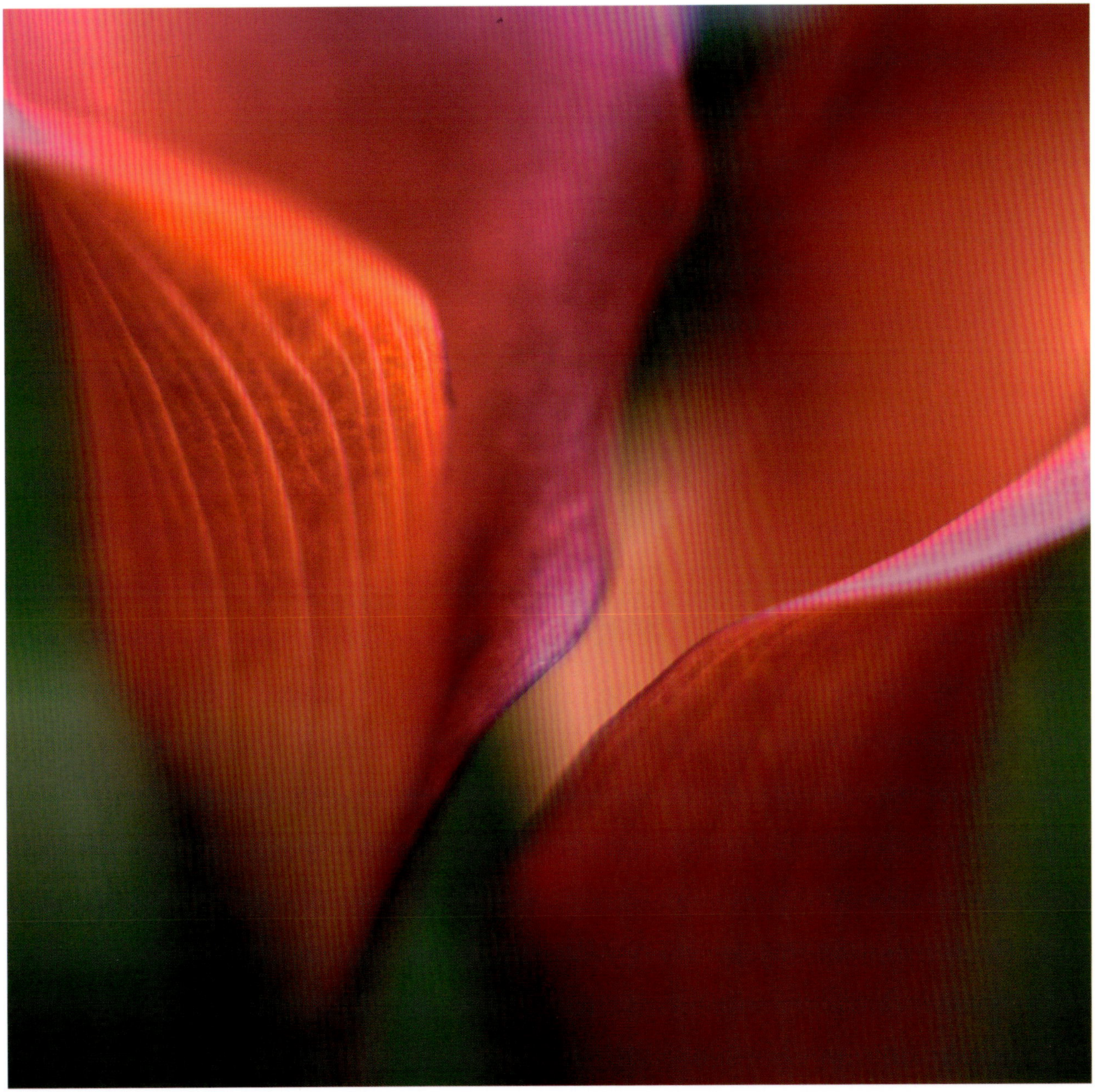

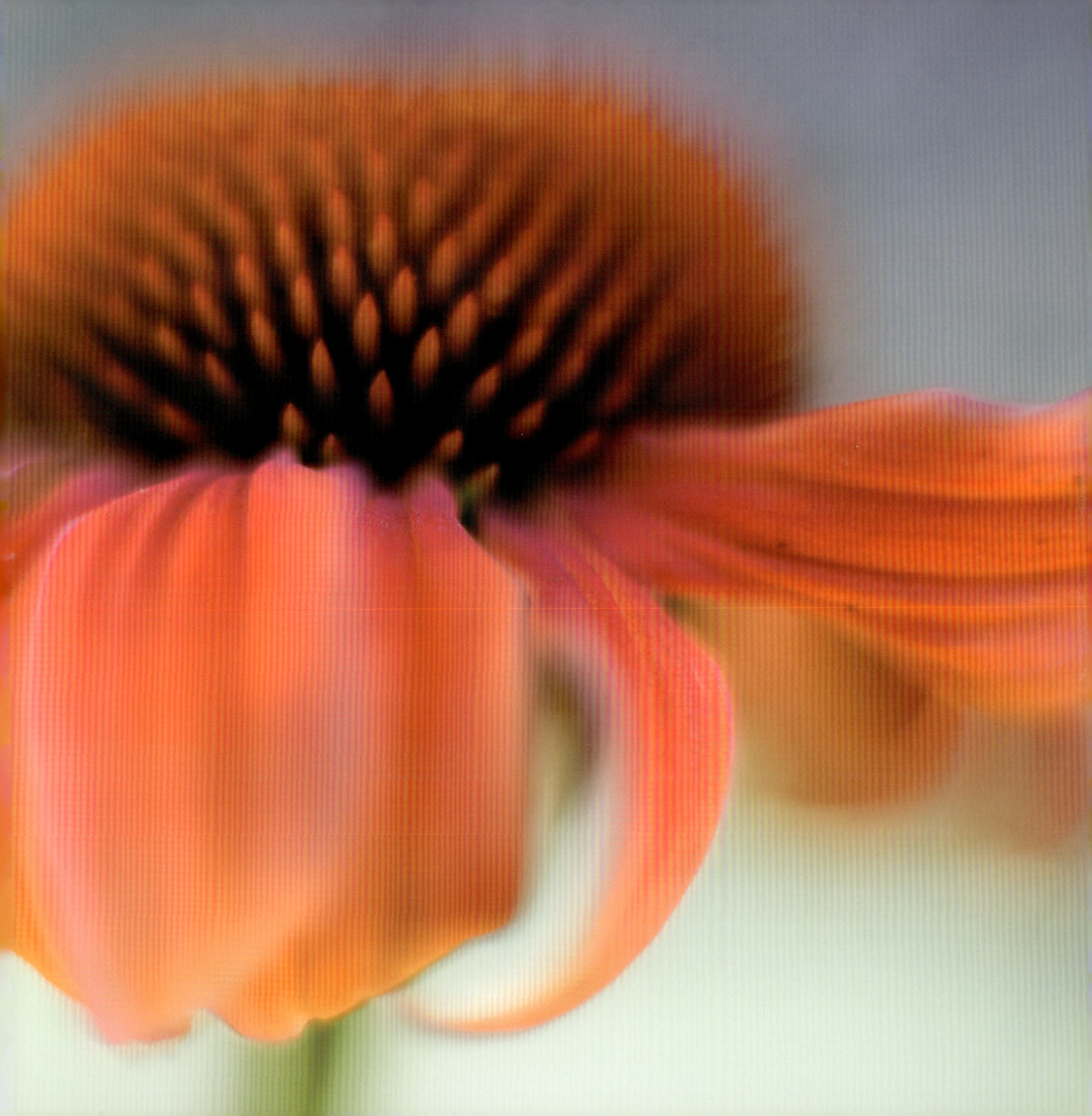

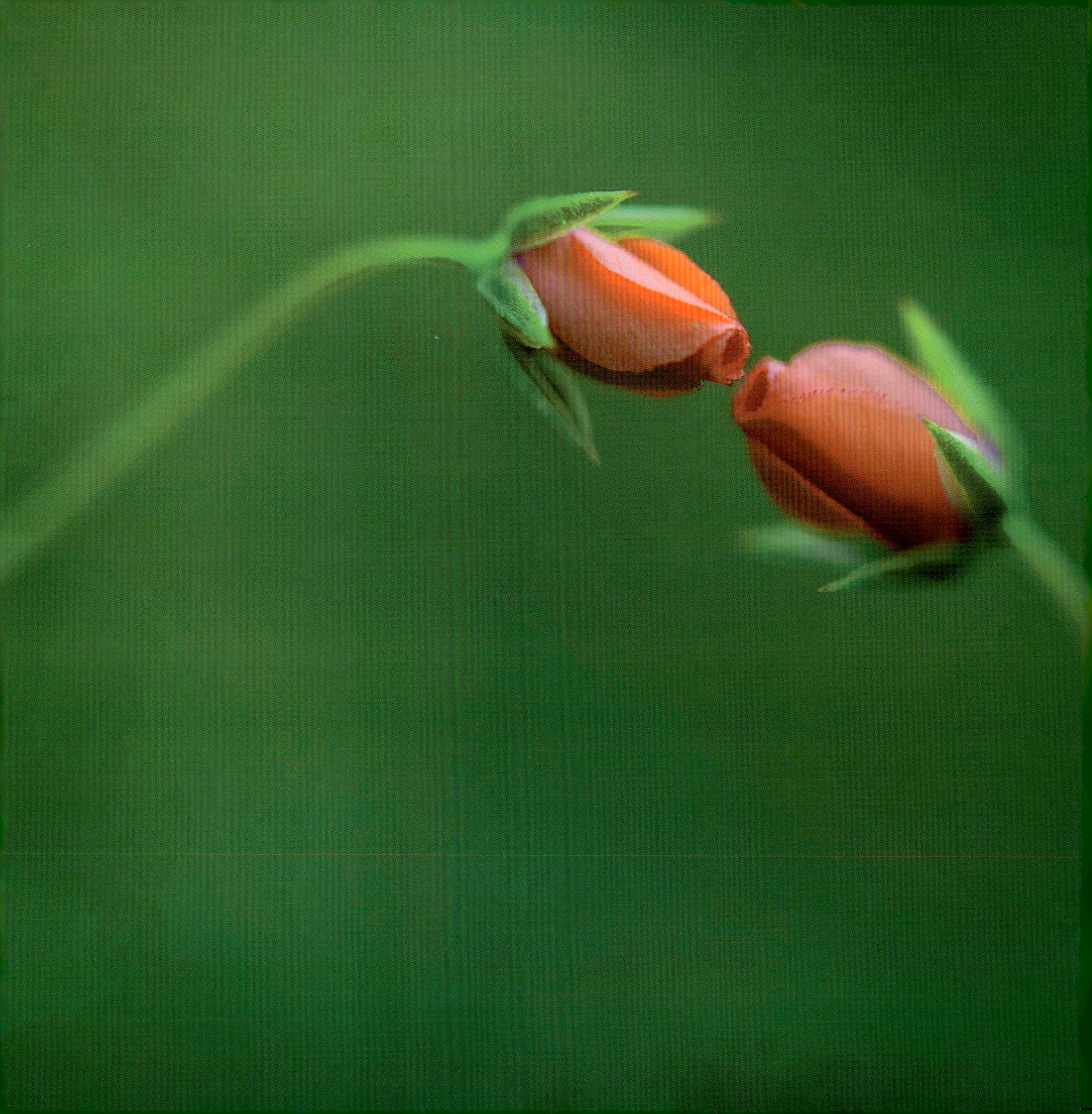

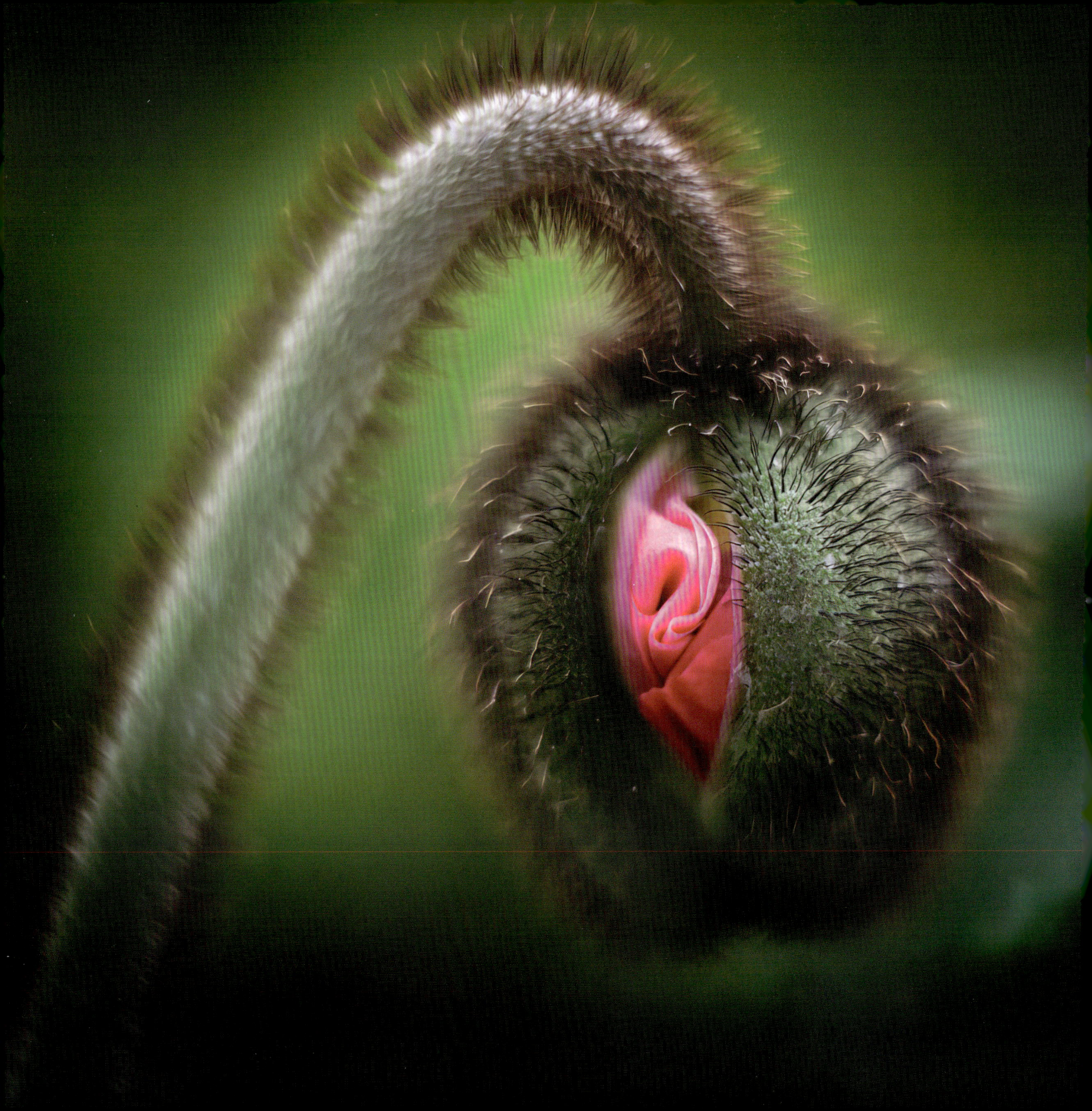

stirrer of desire
provocateur of the erotic
tantalizer with softness and unfolding

Lust is nature's greatest skill.

whatever it takes for procreation—
plants and animals alike

a passerby sees
sighs

Dominatrix!
    Red! savager of modesty
    enticer of sex
    inciter of scandal
    dance partner of passion (tango preferred)

    spewer of lava over old flows
    poppies over meadows

    decorator of lips, the cock's comb
    the butt of baboons, the woman
    walking by—silk across her hips

tulips, roses, amaryllis
poppies, carnations, lilies
poinsettias, huckleberries

    the cape taunting the bull
    poisonous snake
    poisonous frog

You are blood
bleeding out in war
feeding the child in the womb.

Be careful with my heart!

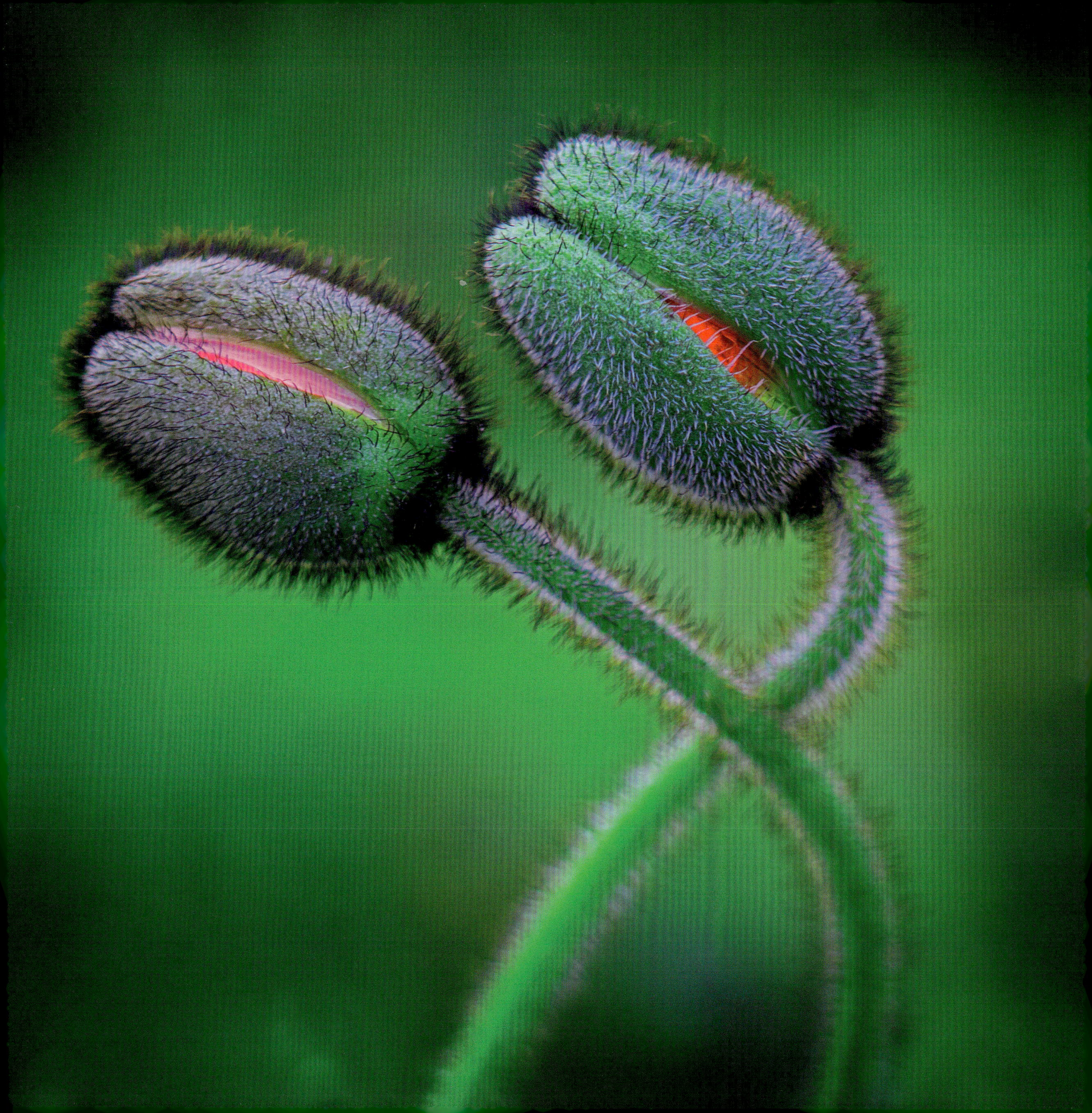

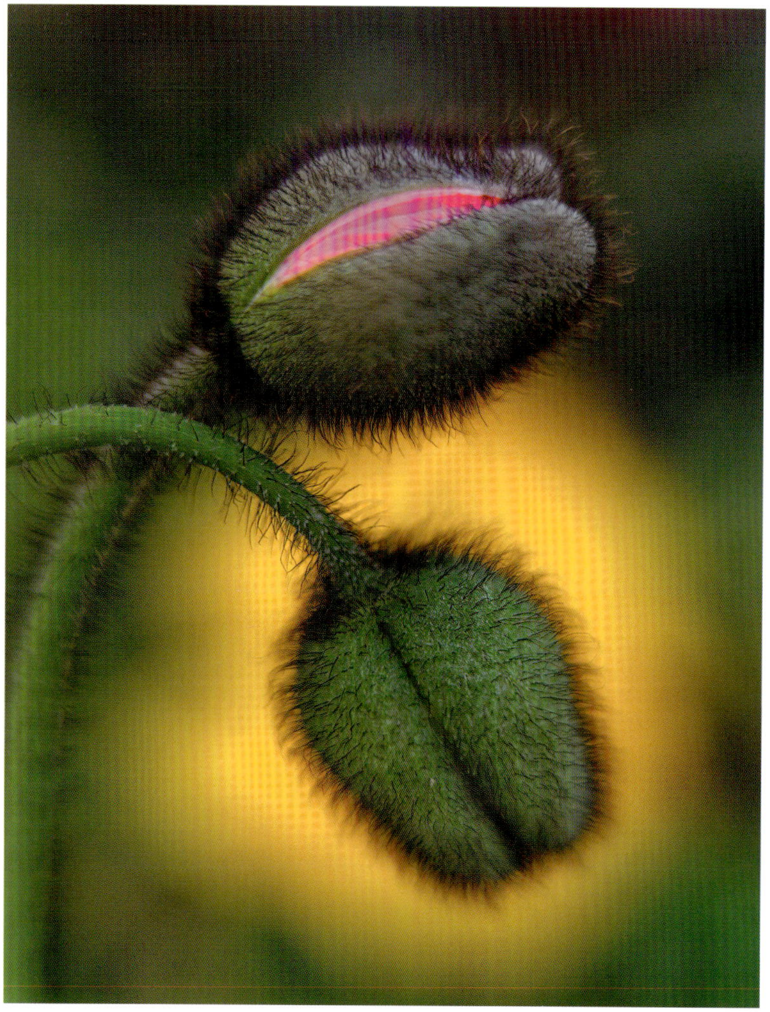

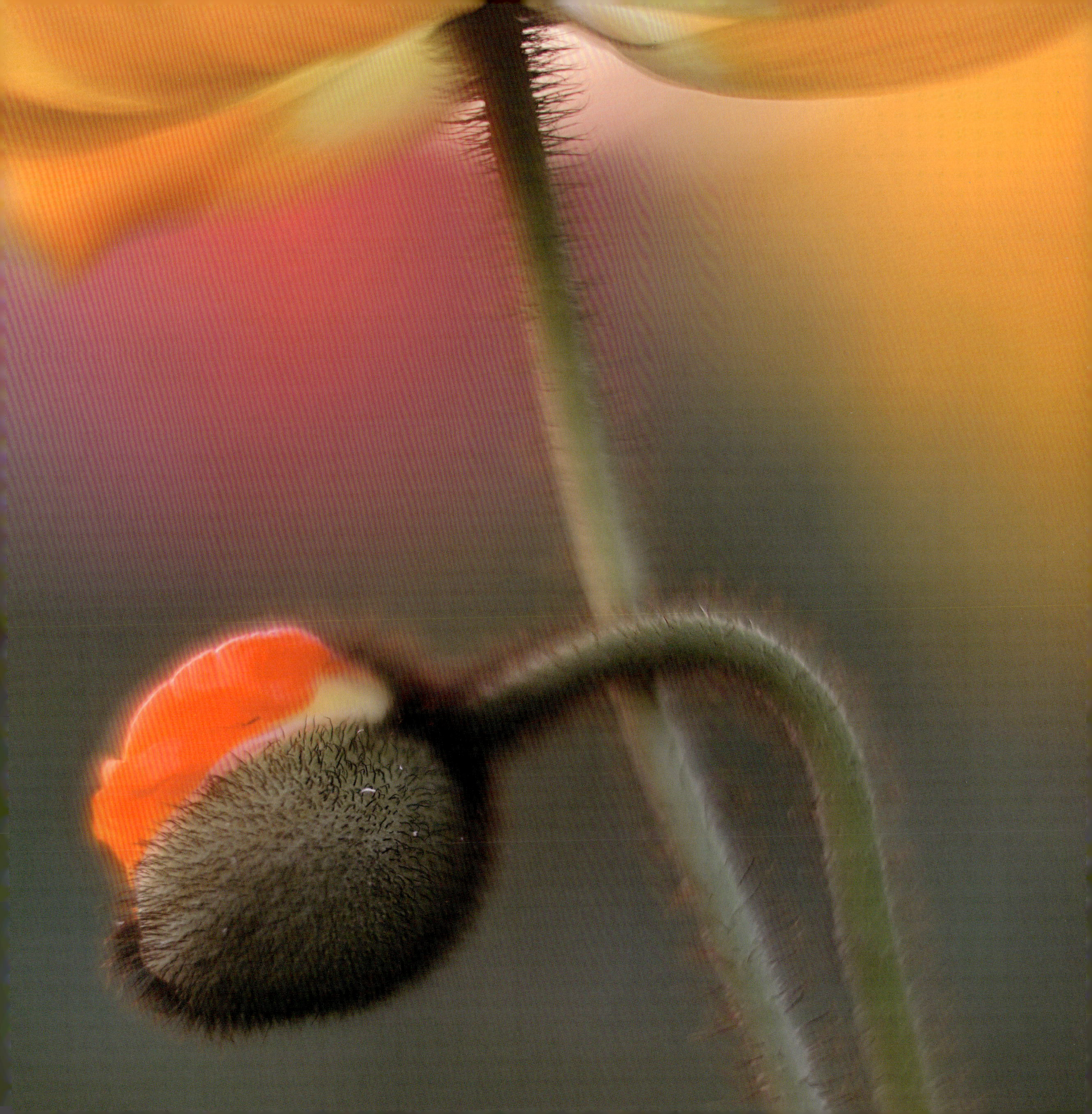

Flowers are silent —

no chime from their bells
no song from their trumpets
no percussion from their leaves

Why, then, do I hear music?

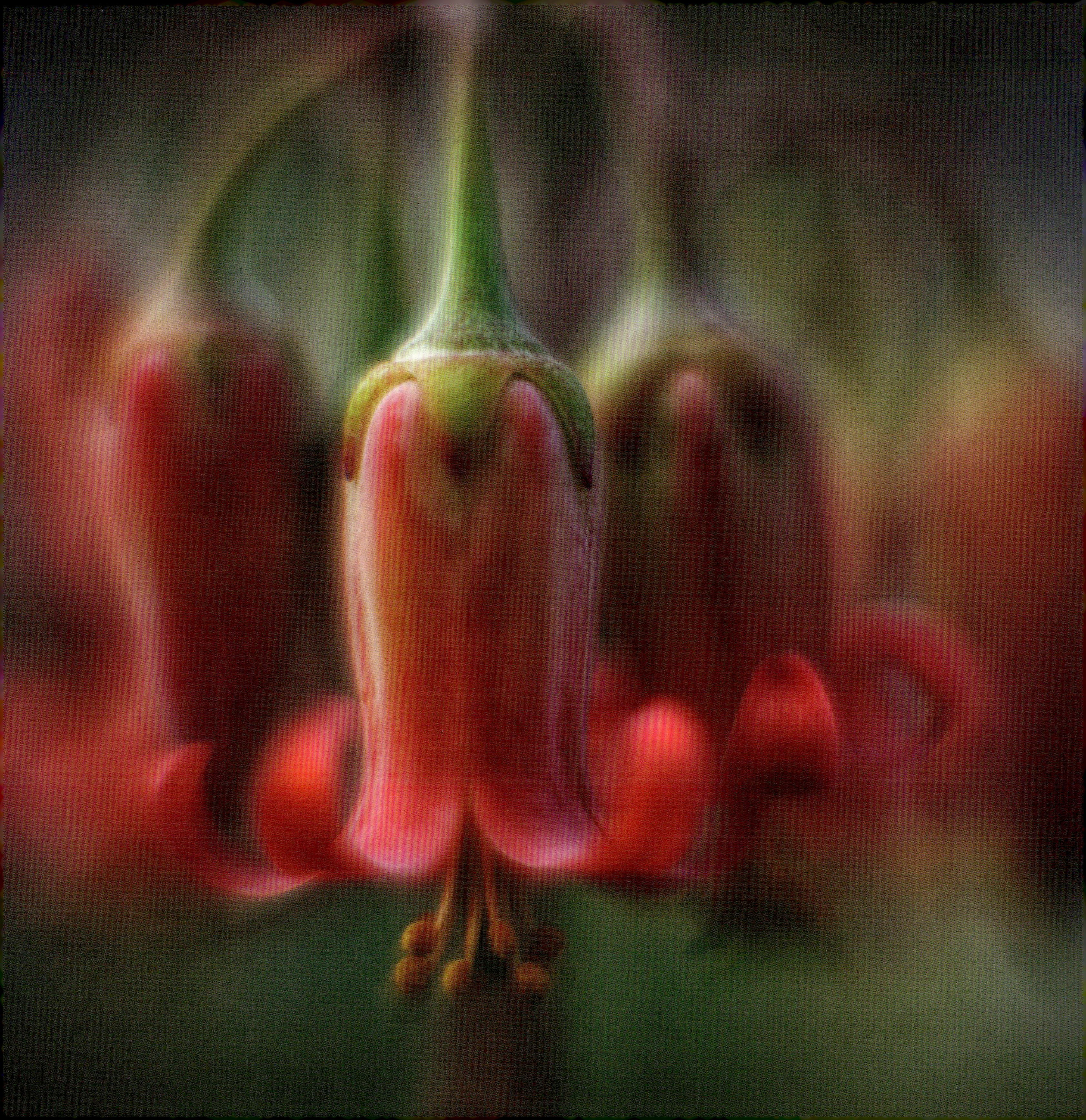

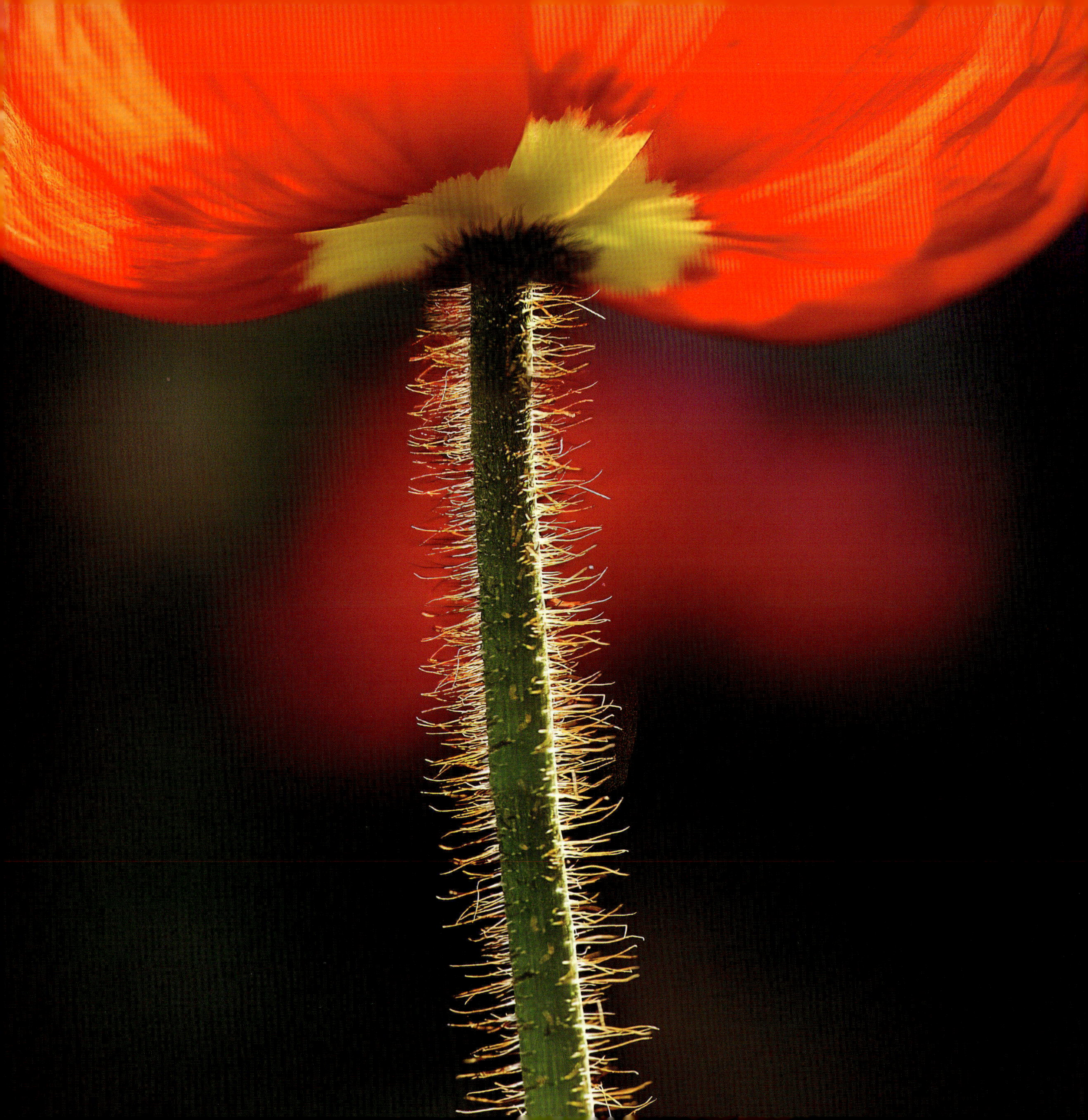

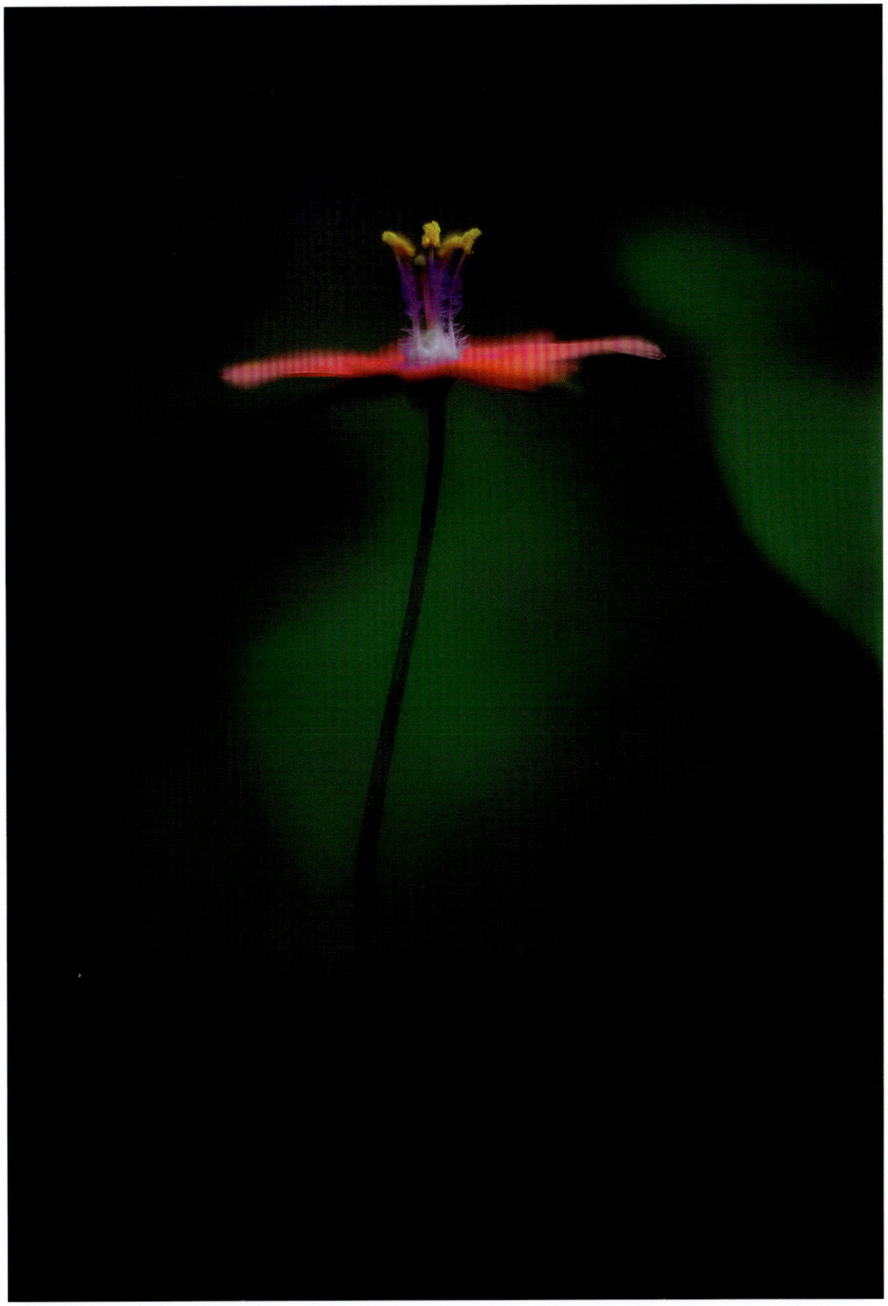

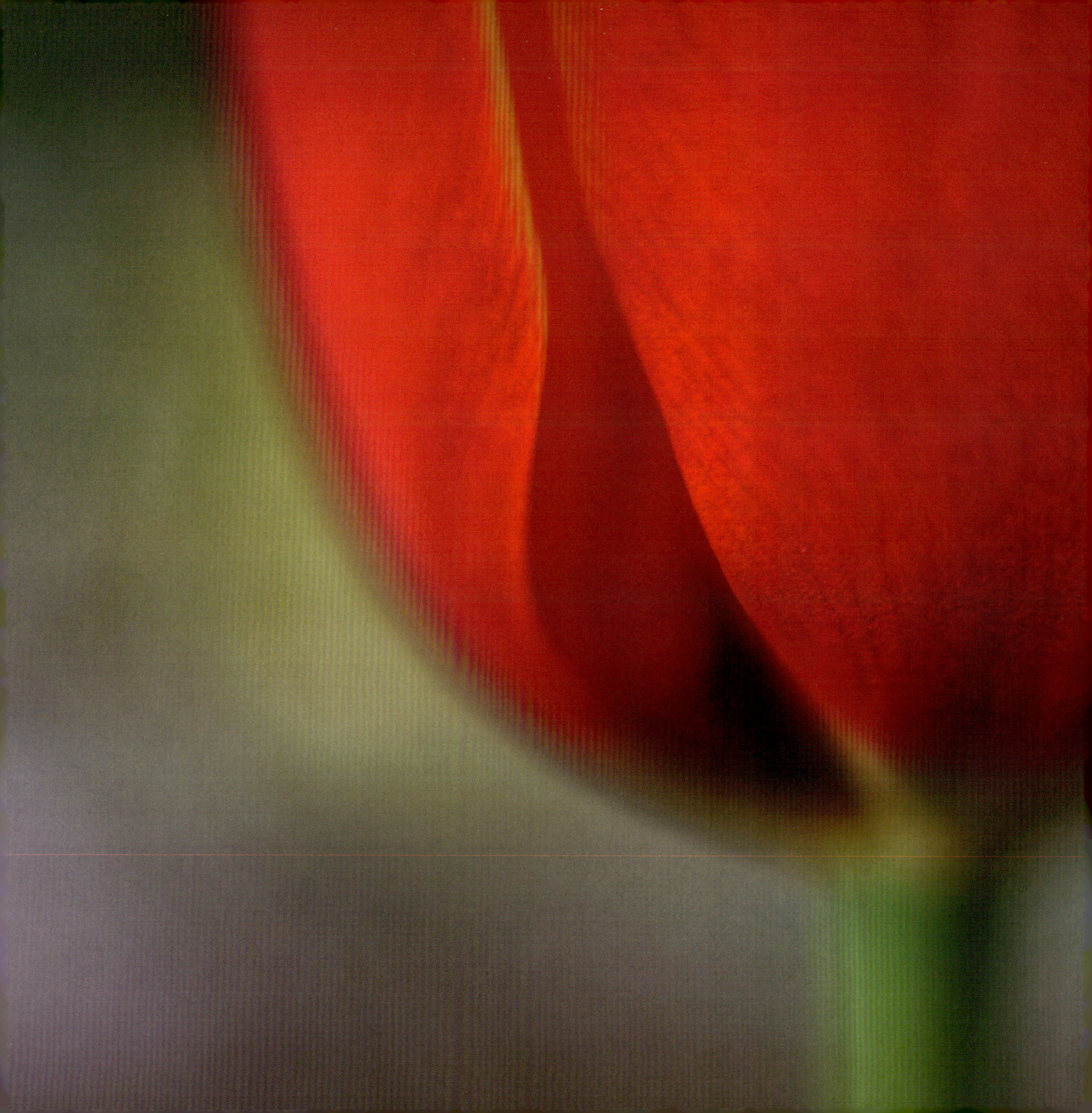

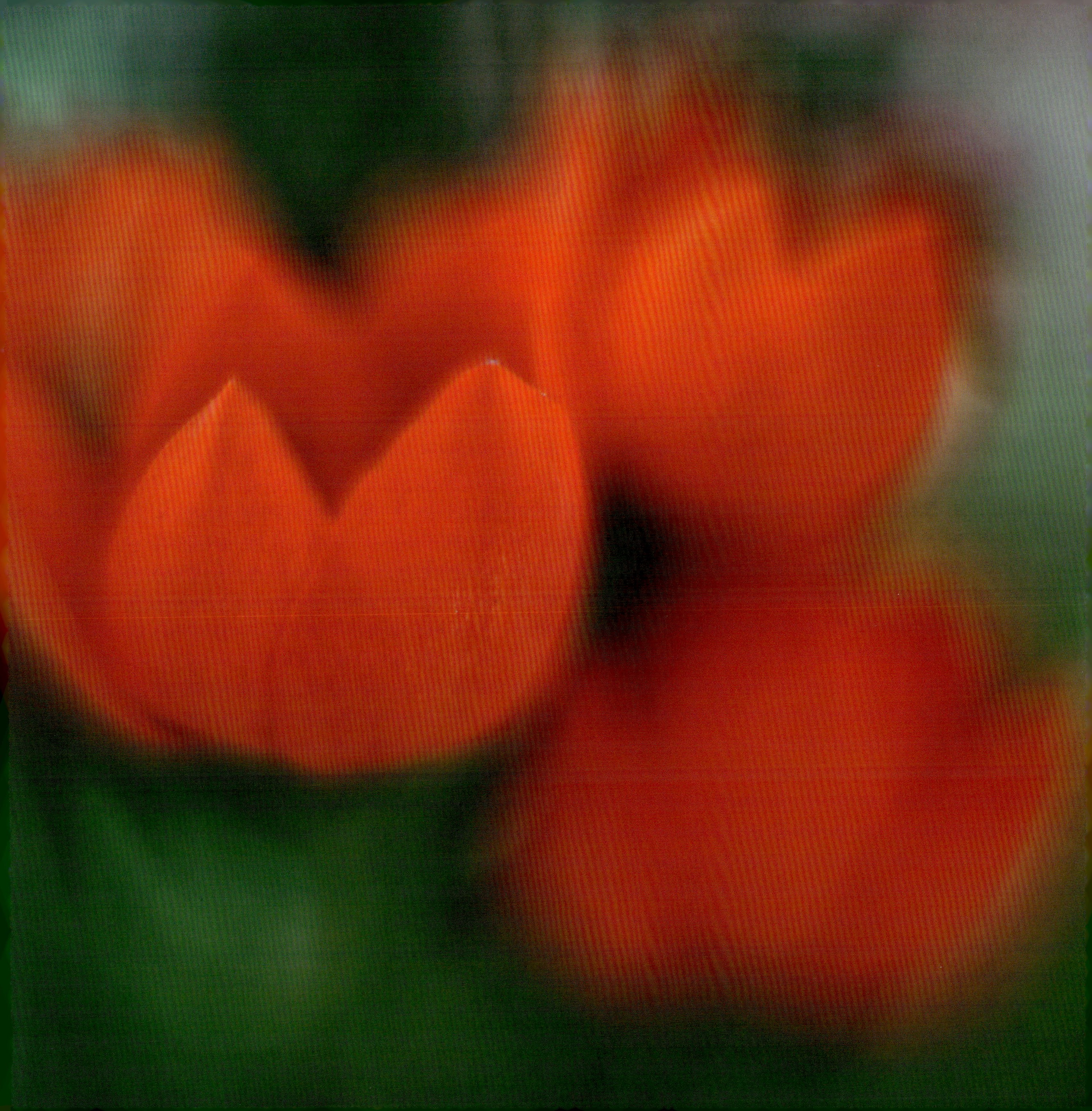

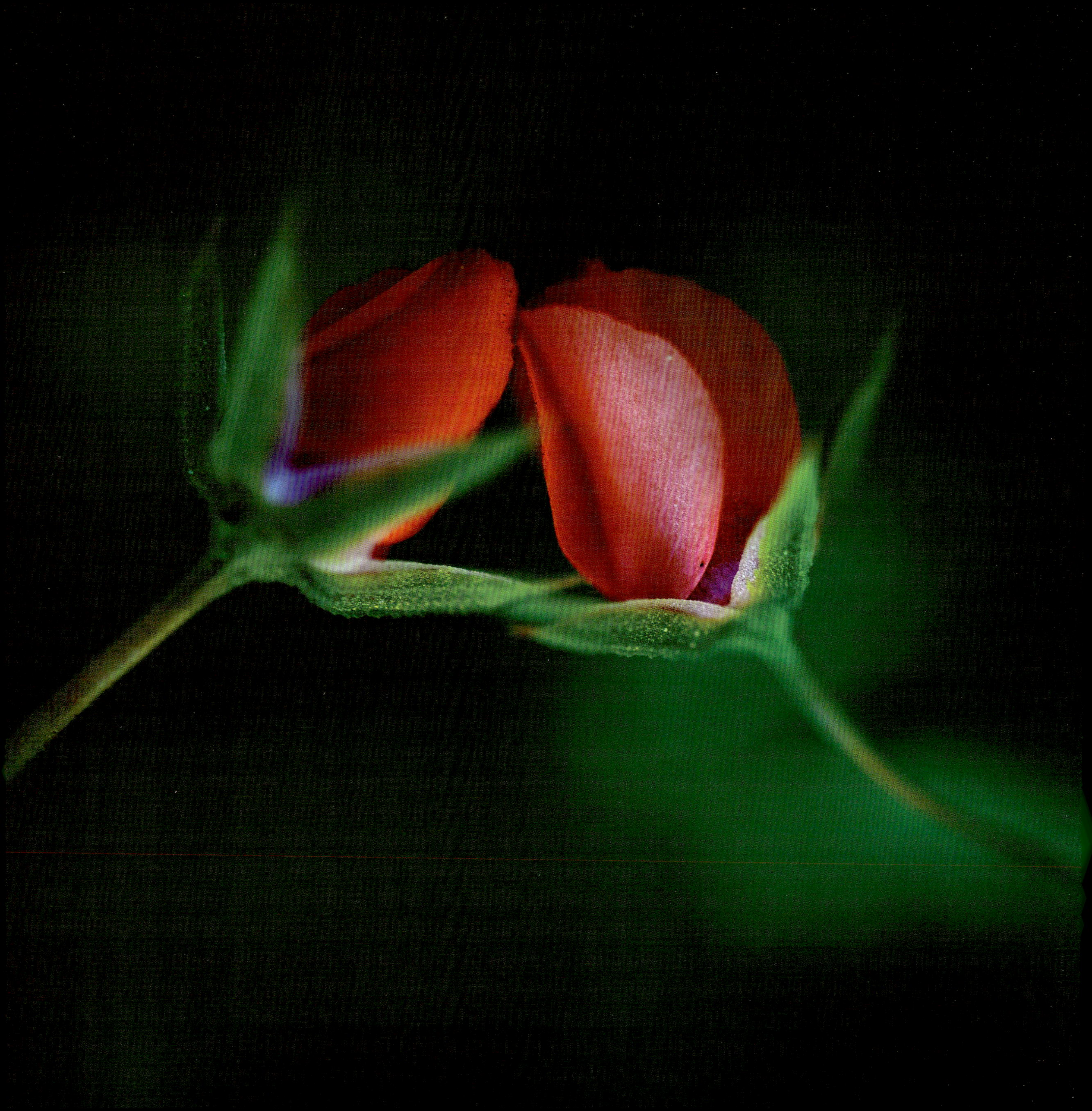

I prefer delicate seduction
and to greet the morning at first warmth
with the wren.

We are alike, the wren and I
    easy to overlook
    passionate beyond our size.

You will not forget me.

You will remember when humbled
and searching again for quiet grace.

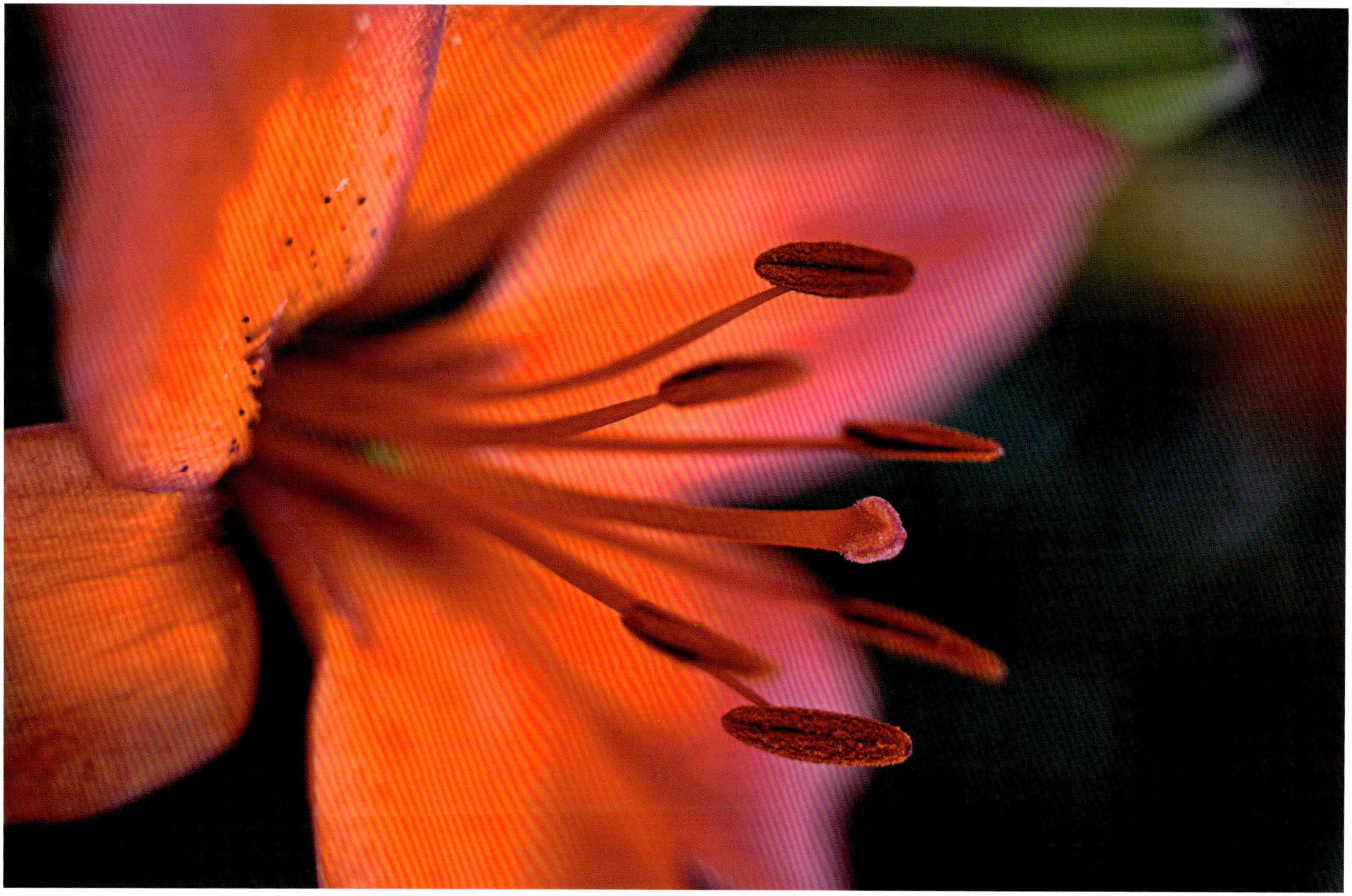

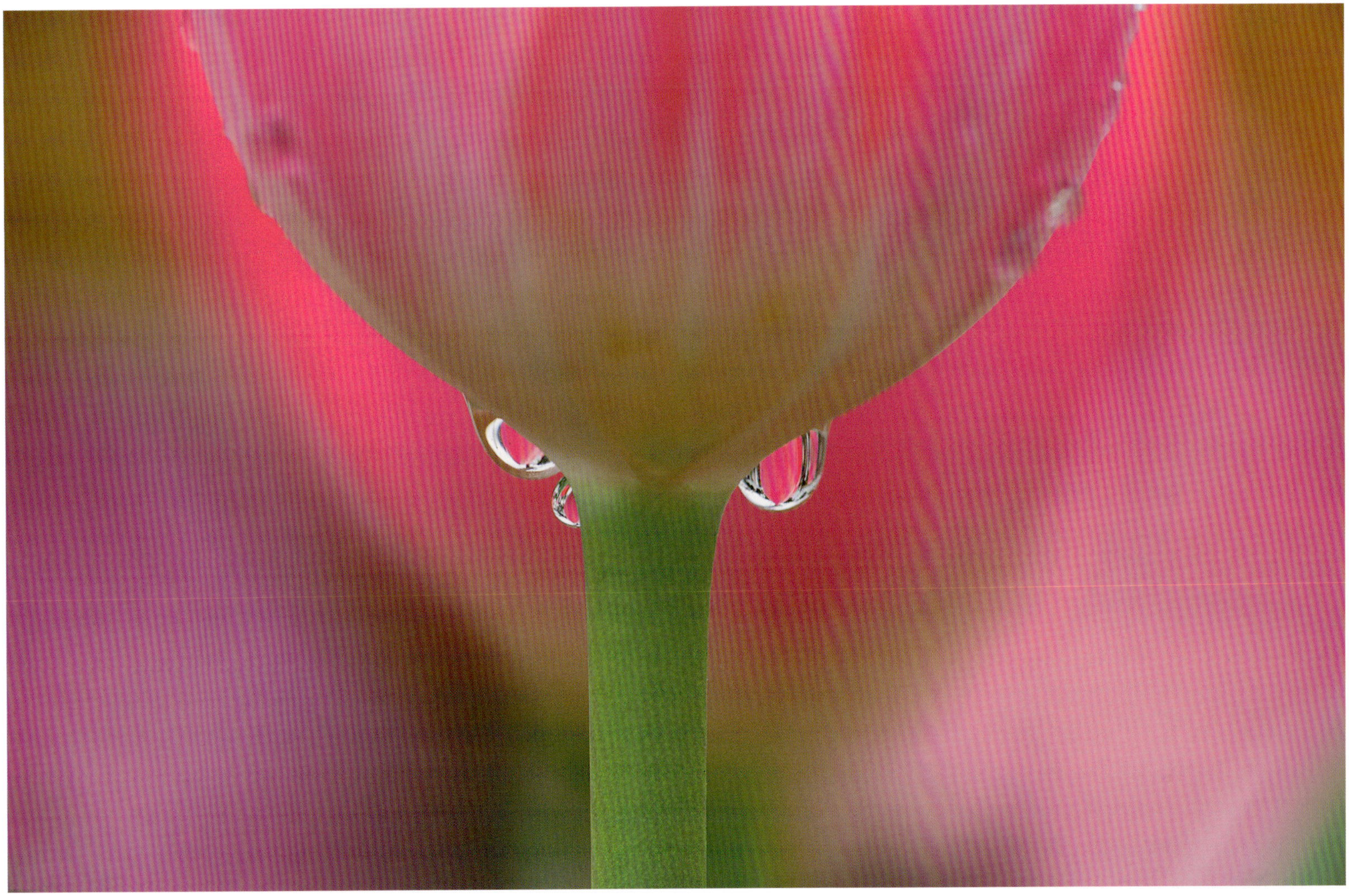

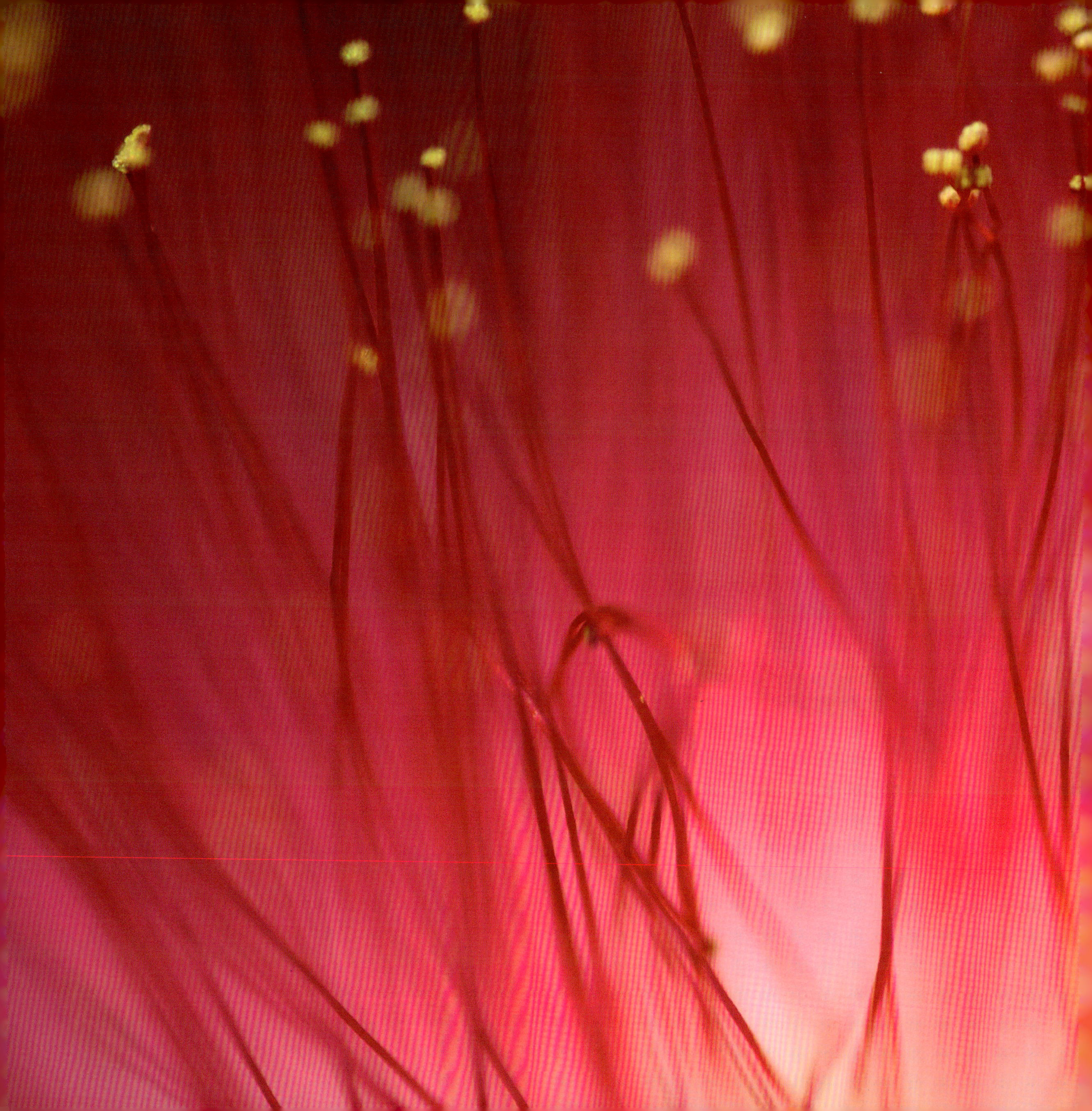

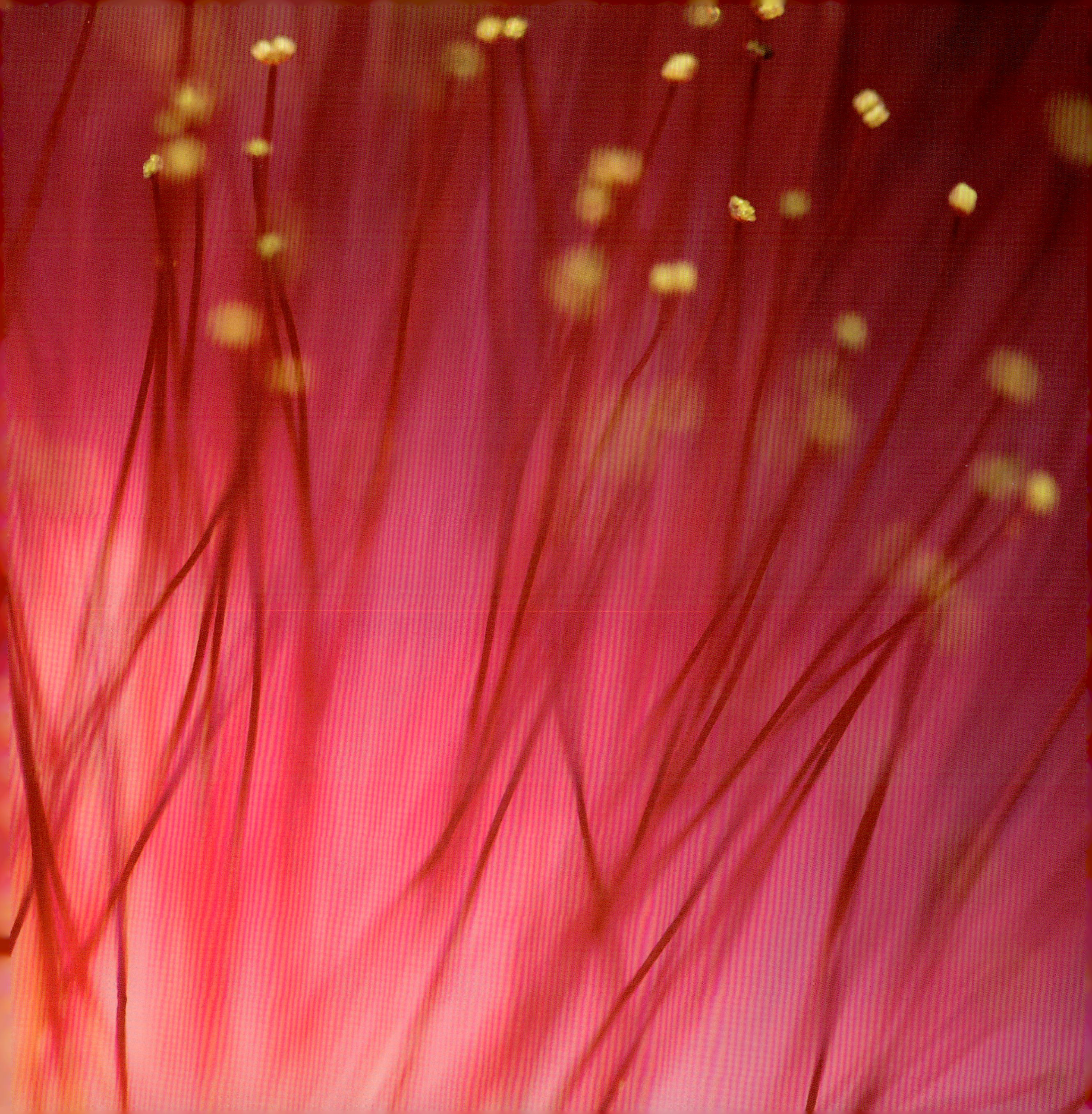

First dark, then warmth and wet,
dig of root, thrust of stem

claims made on earth and sun
for leaf, petal, stamen, bud,
pollen, bloom, color, scent

A visitor flutters, pierces, mines.

There will be honey.

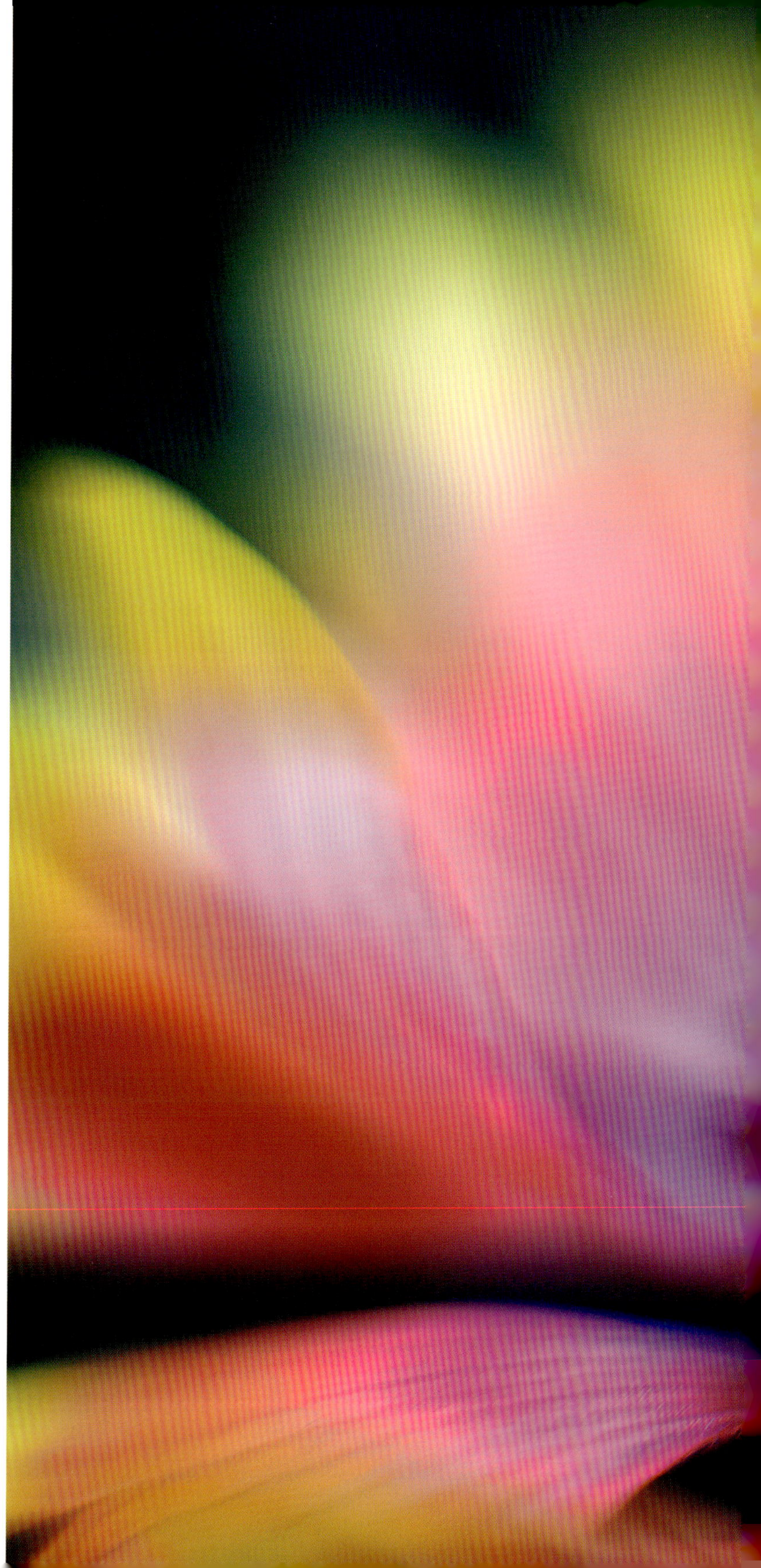

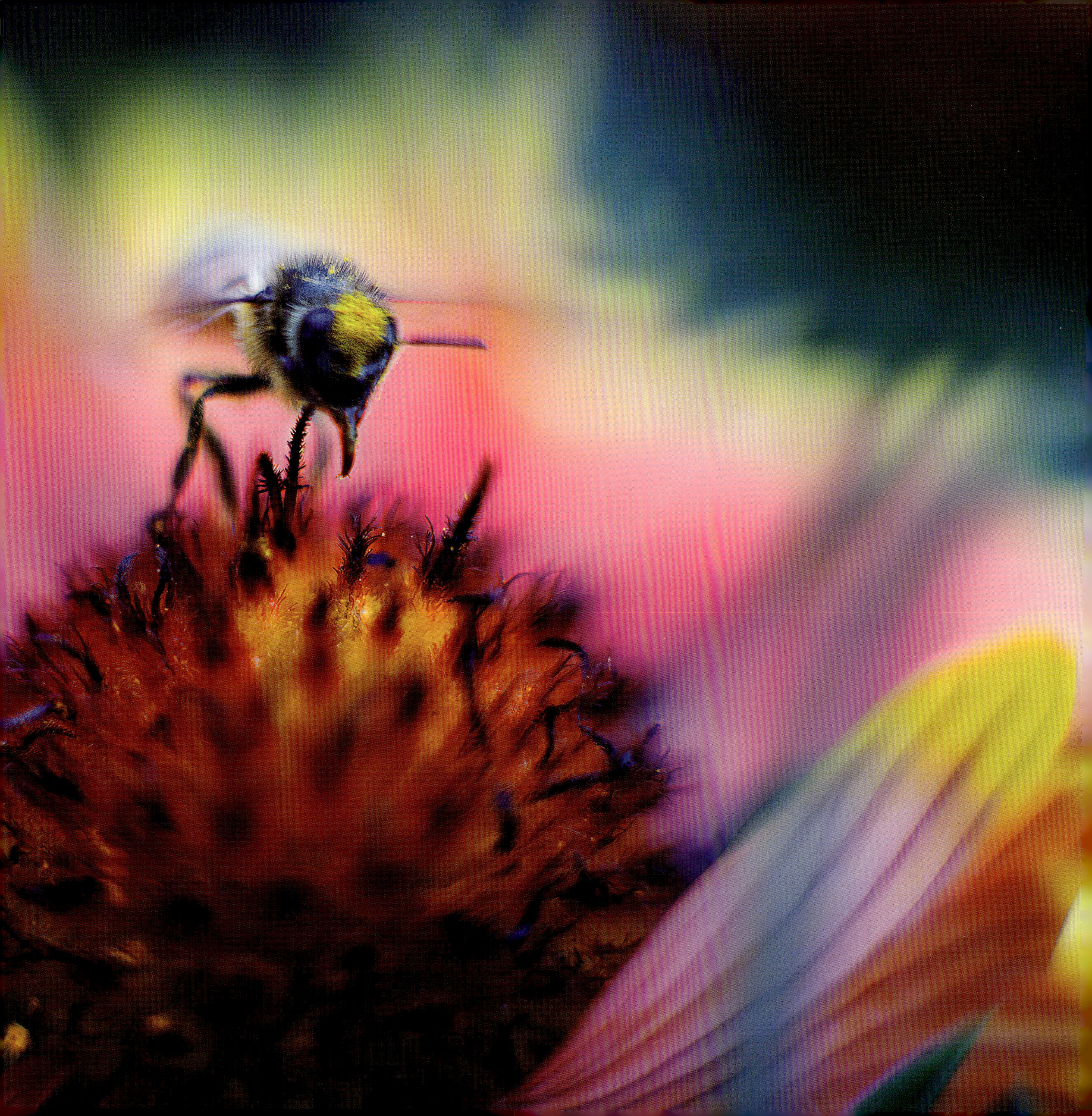

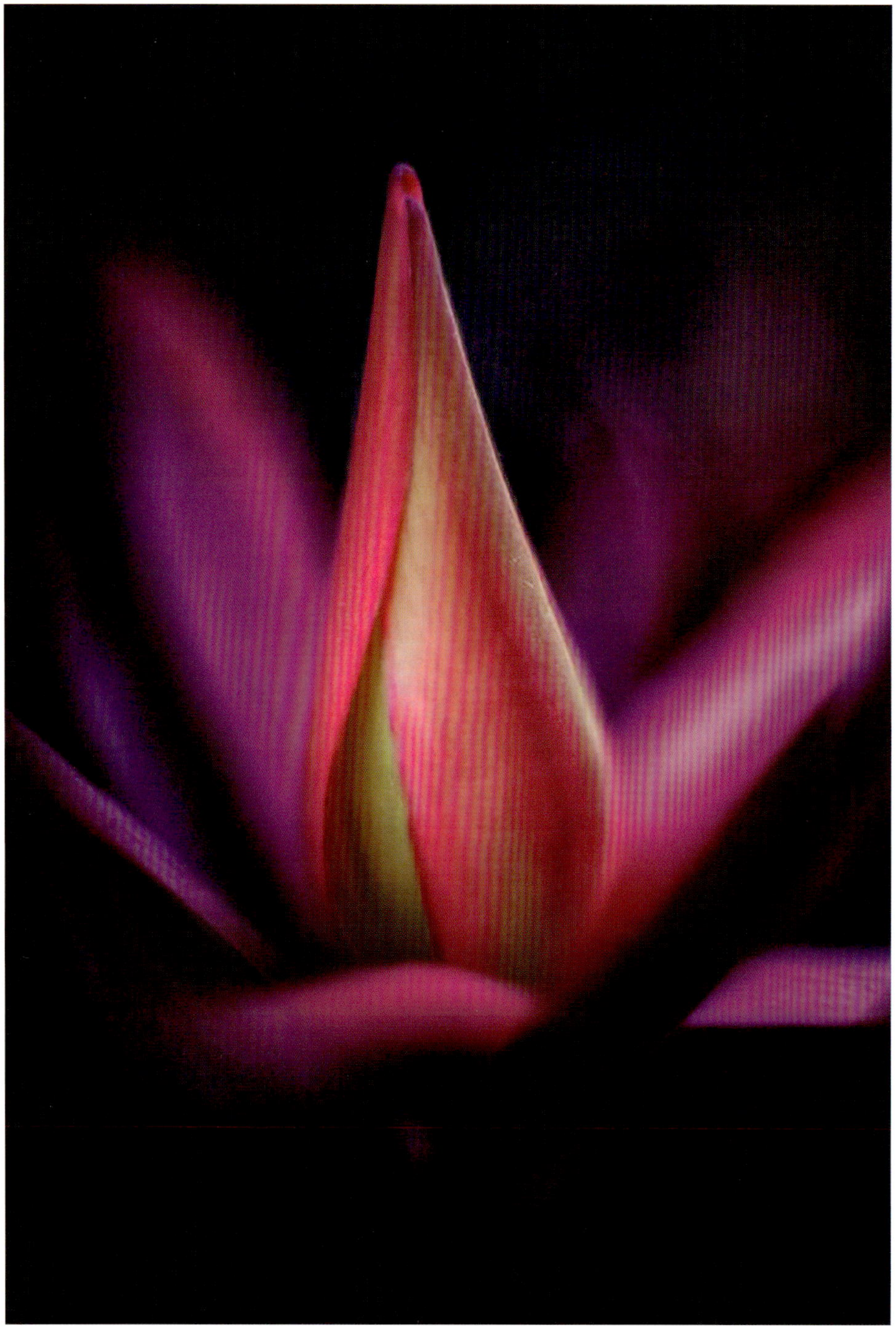

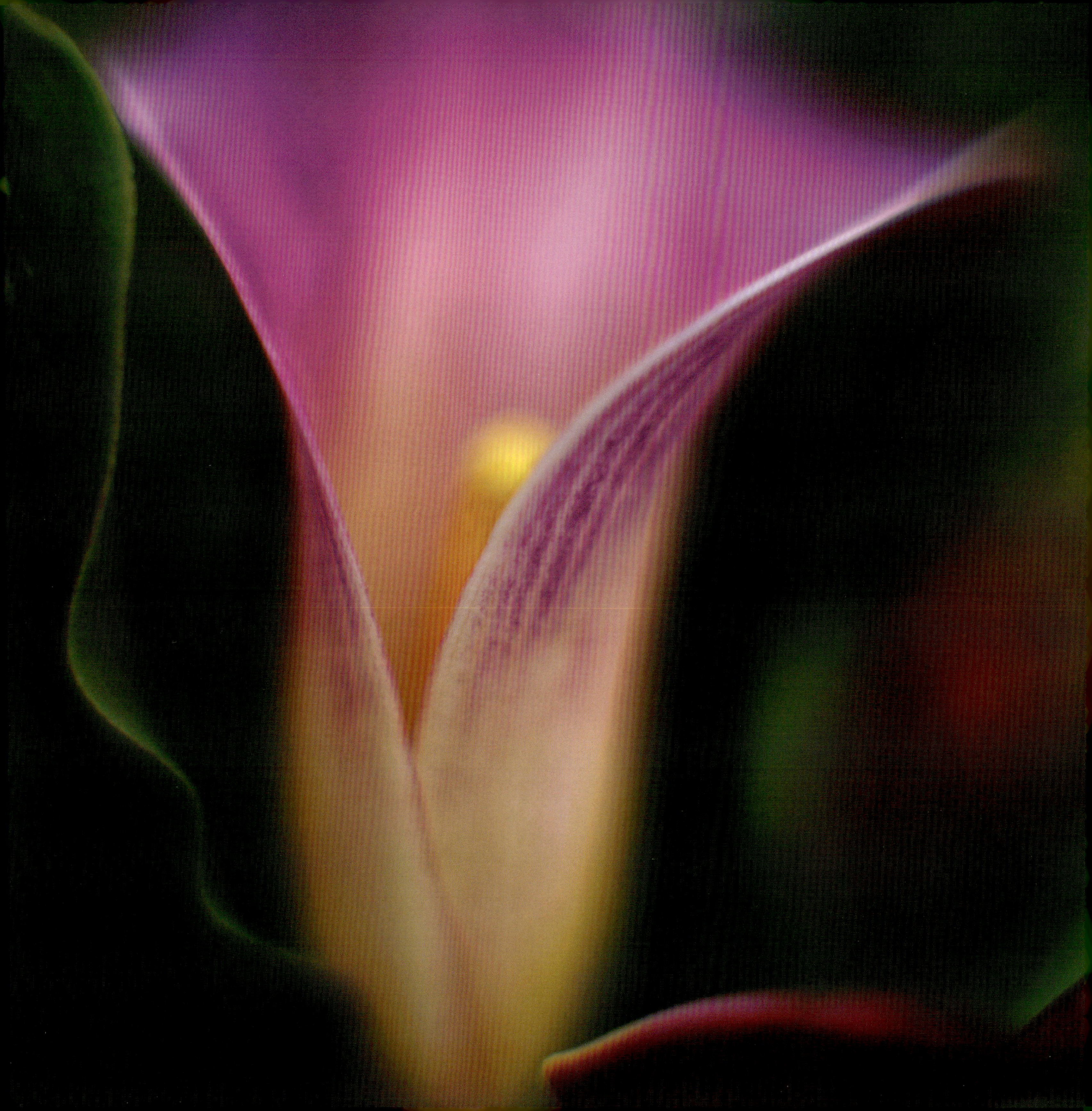

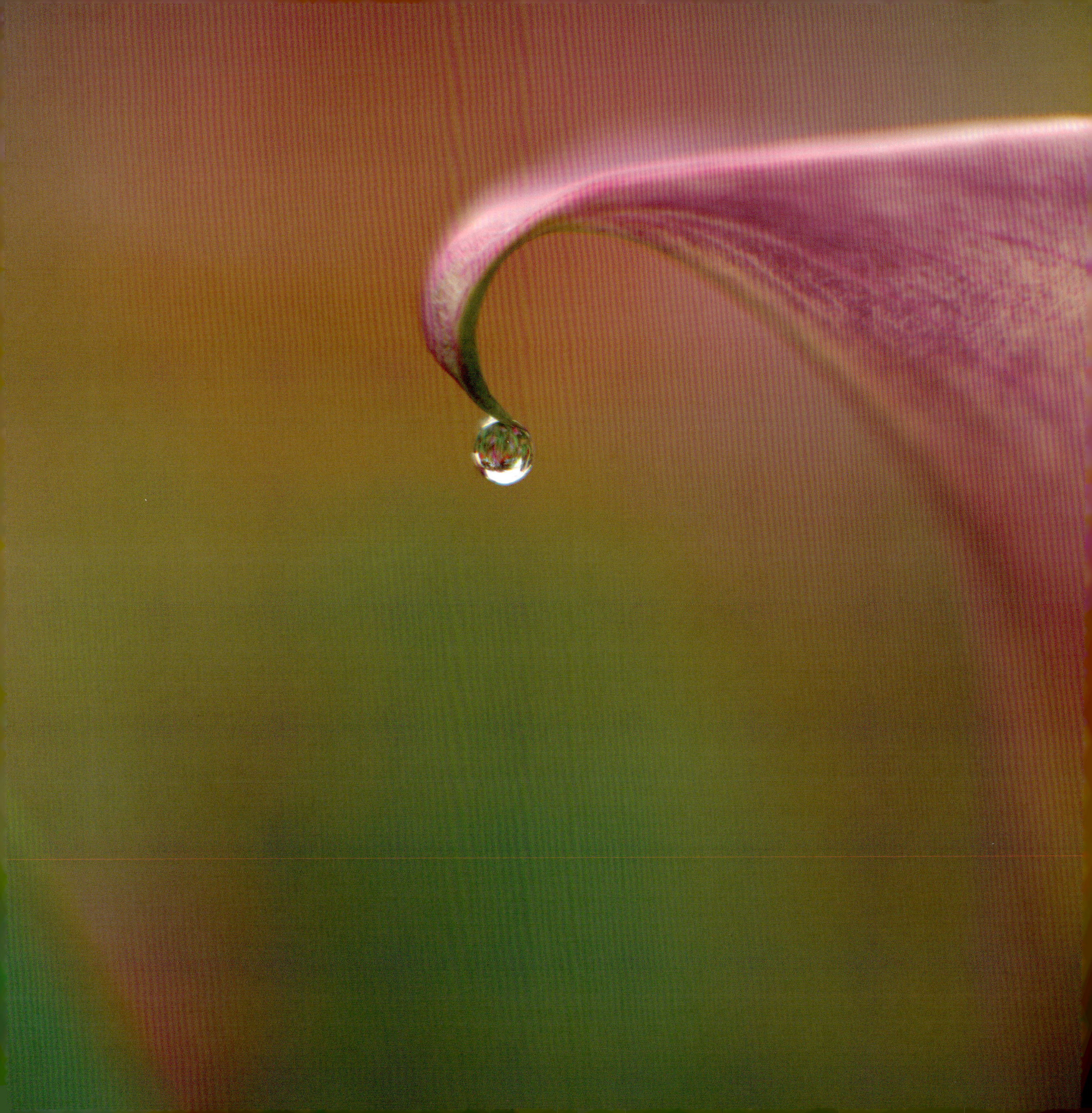

The average flower is 90% water.

No flower is average.

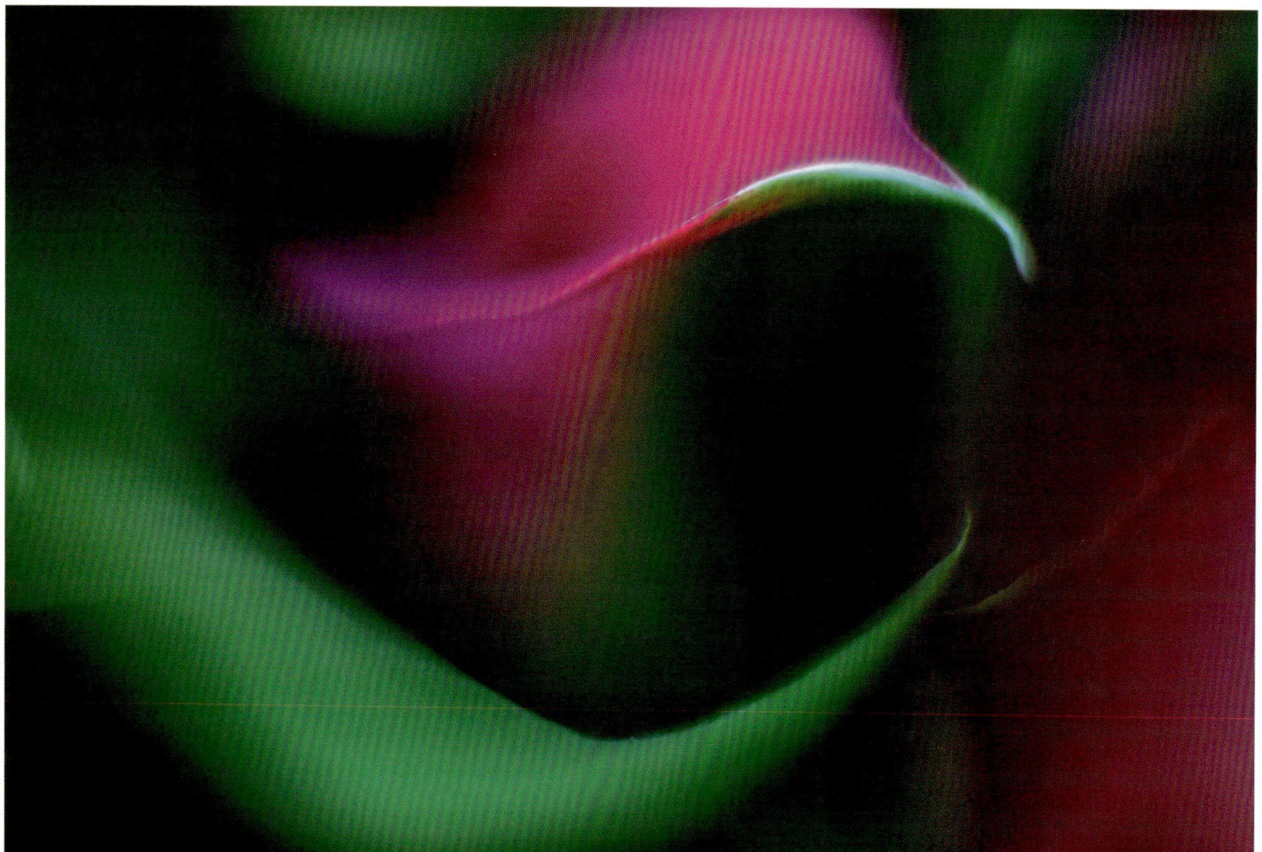

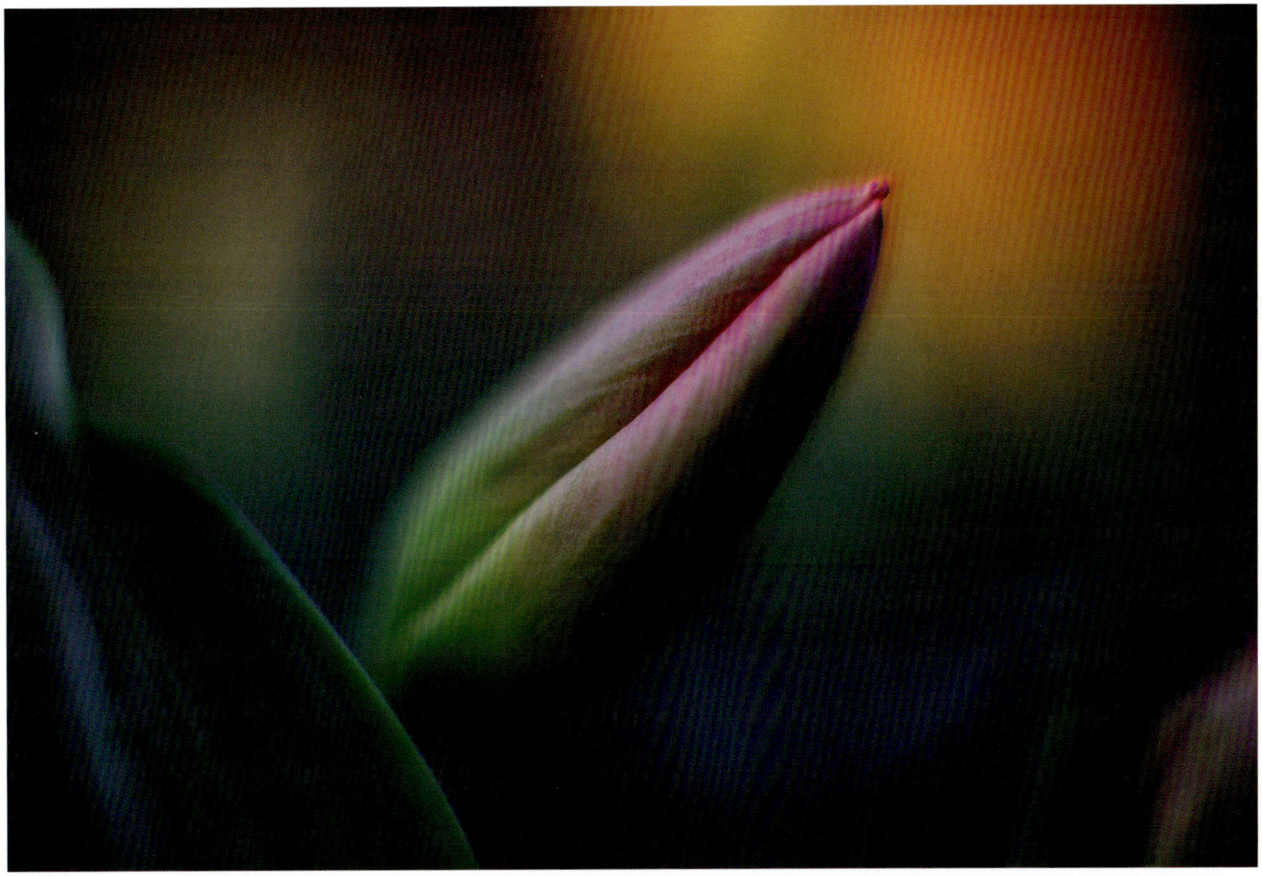

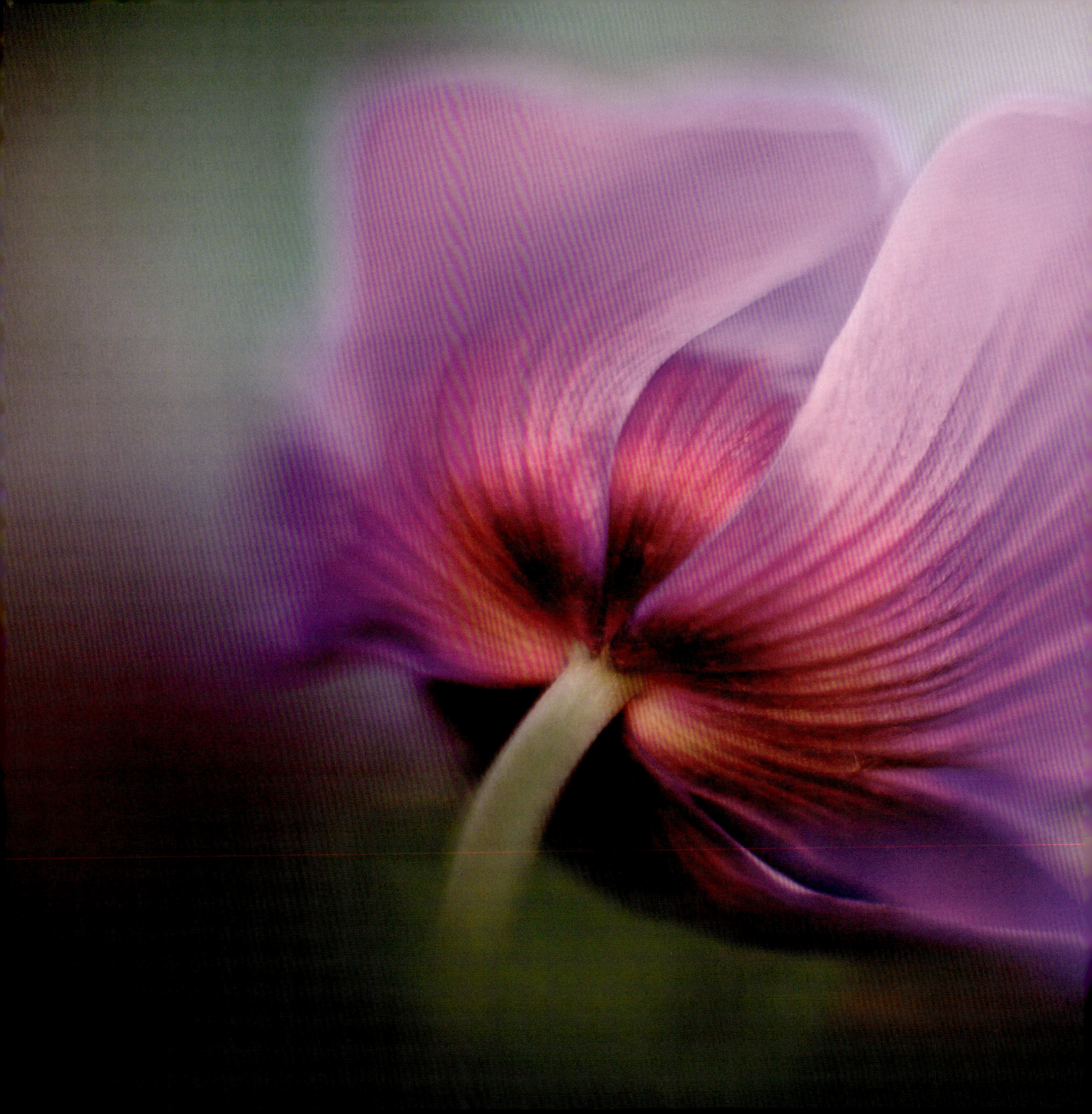

Touch me so gently
we become everything
and one.

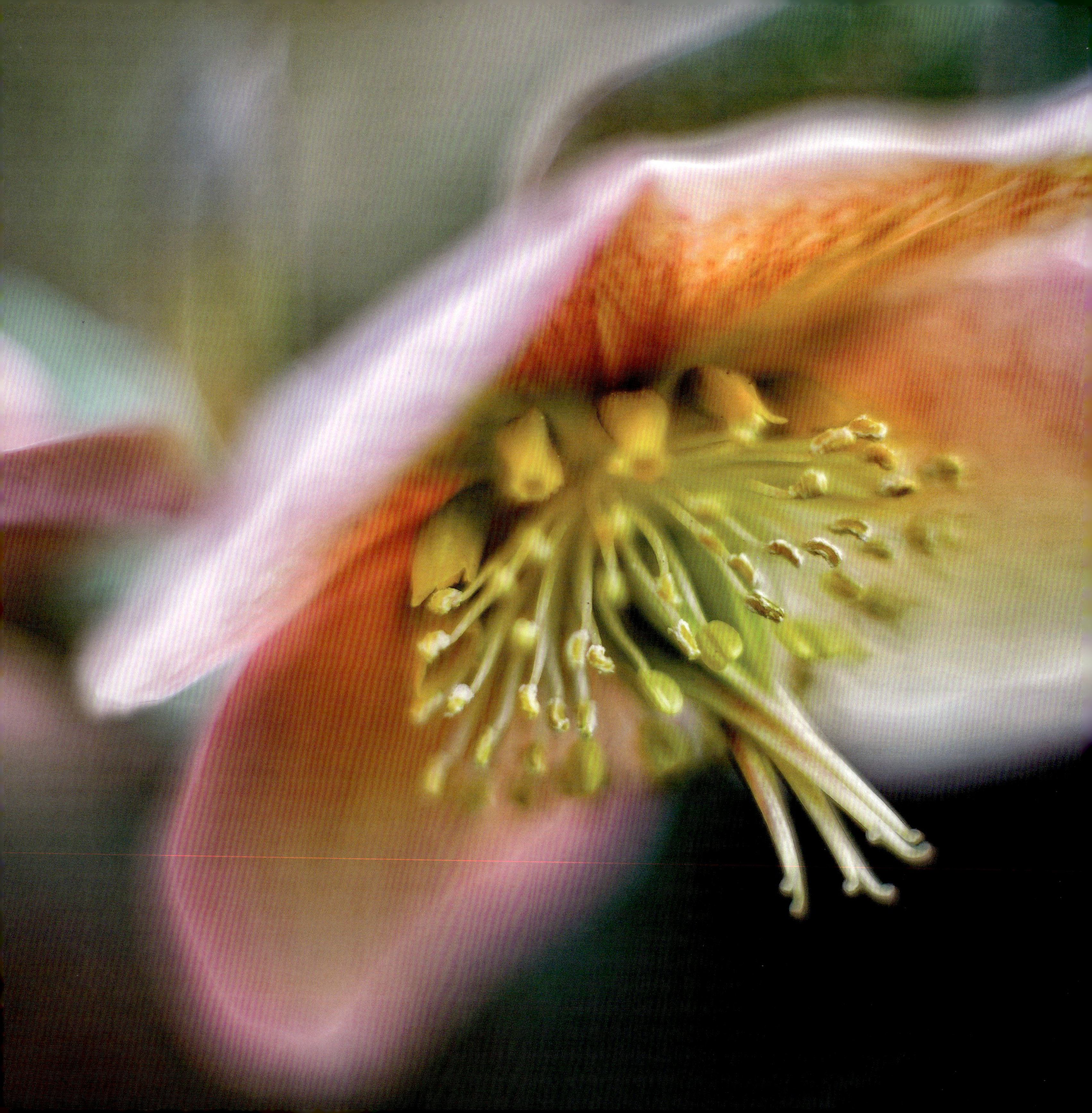

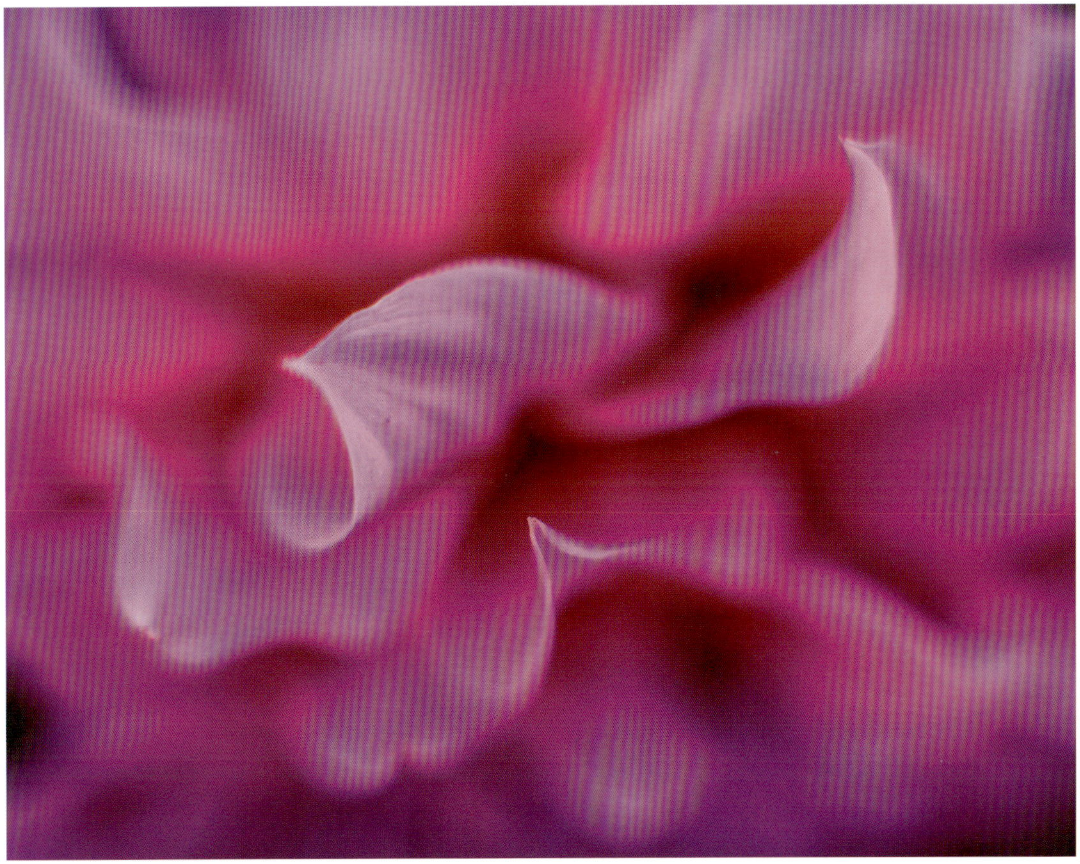

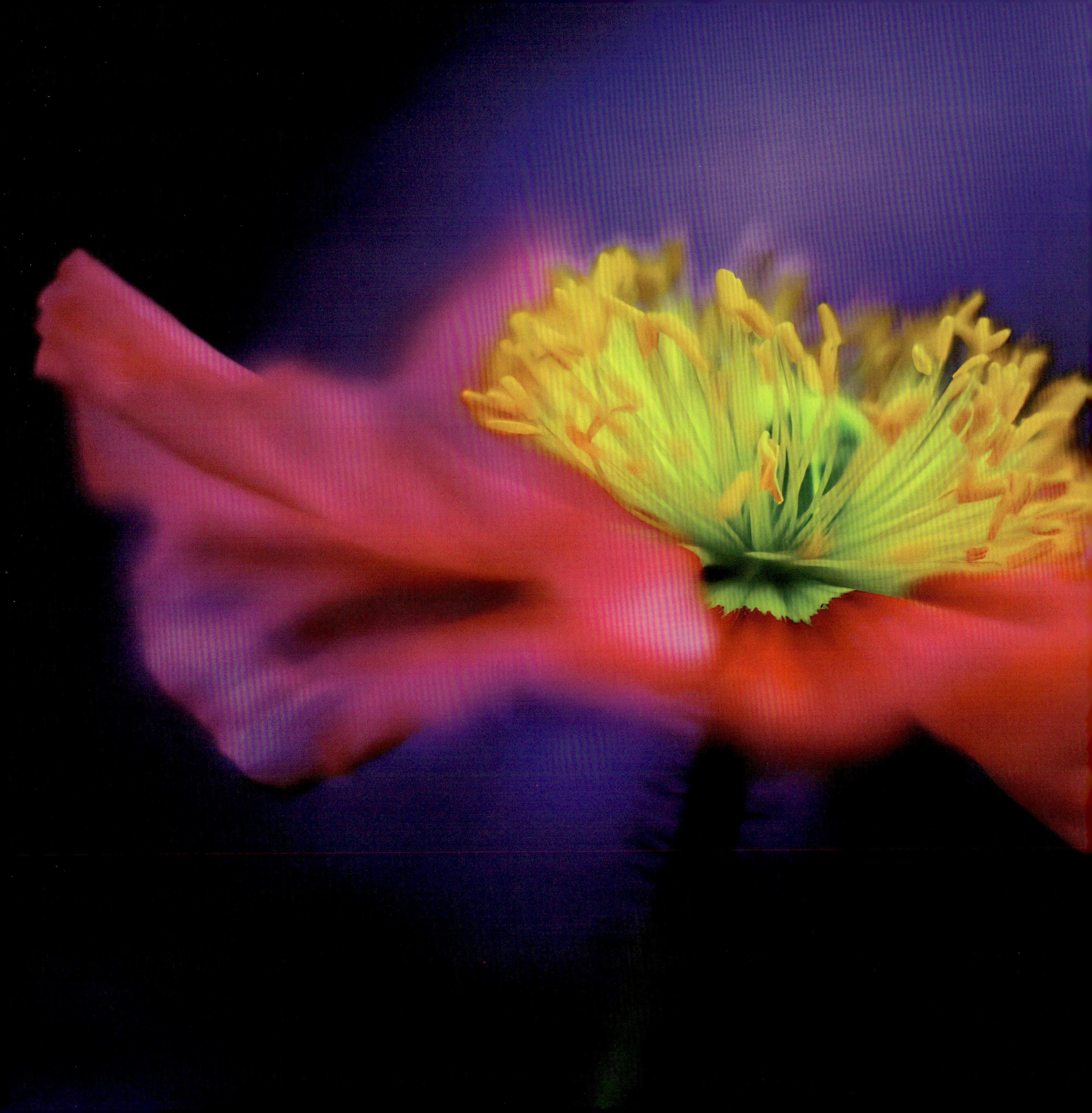

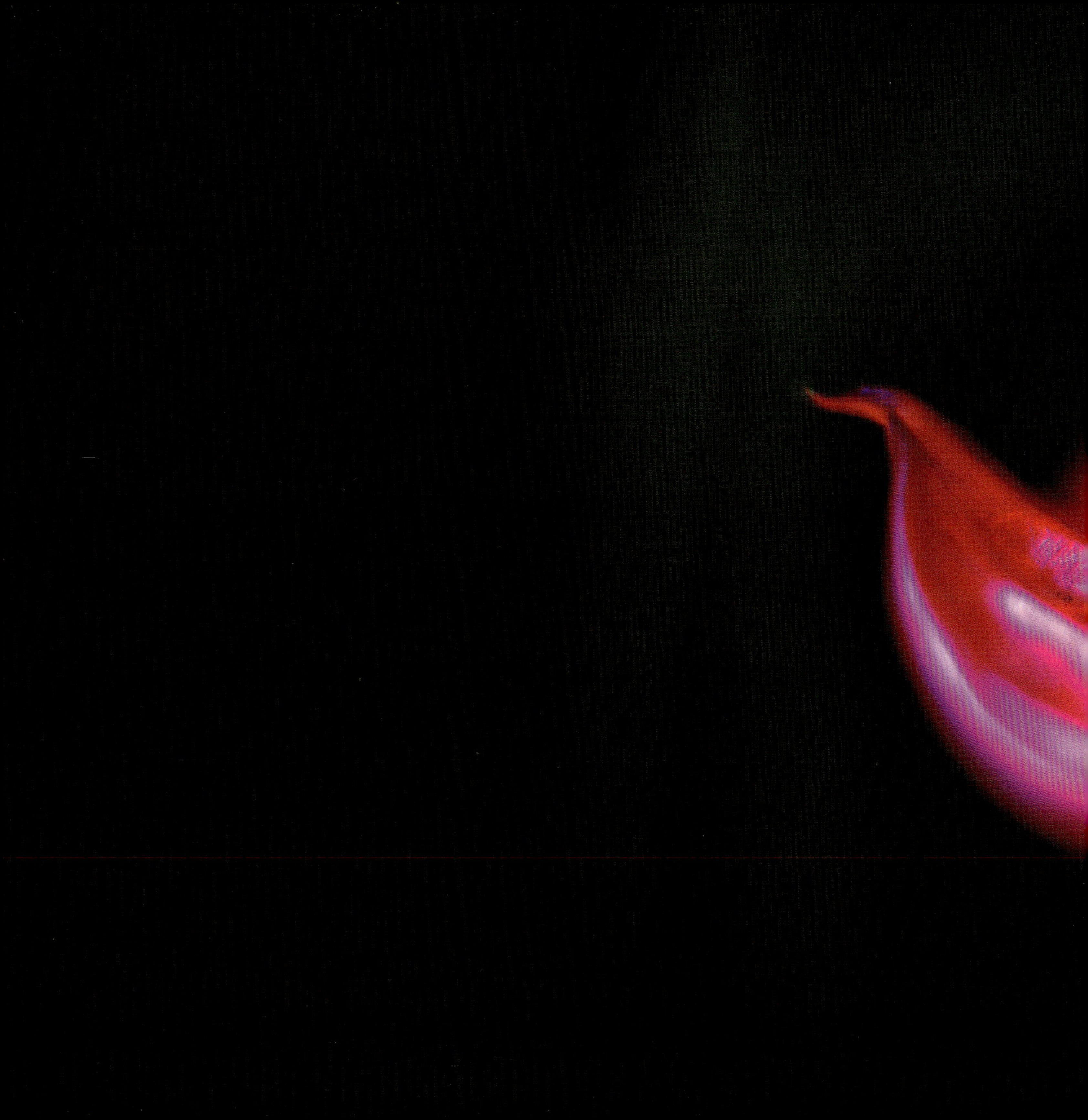

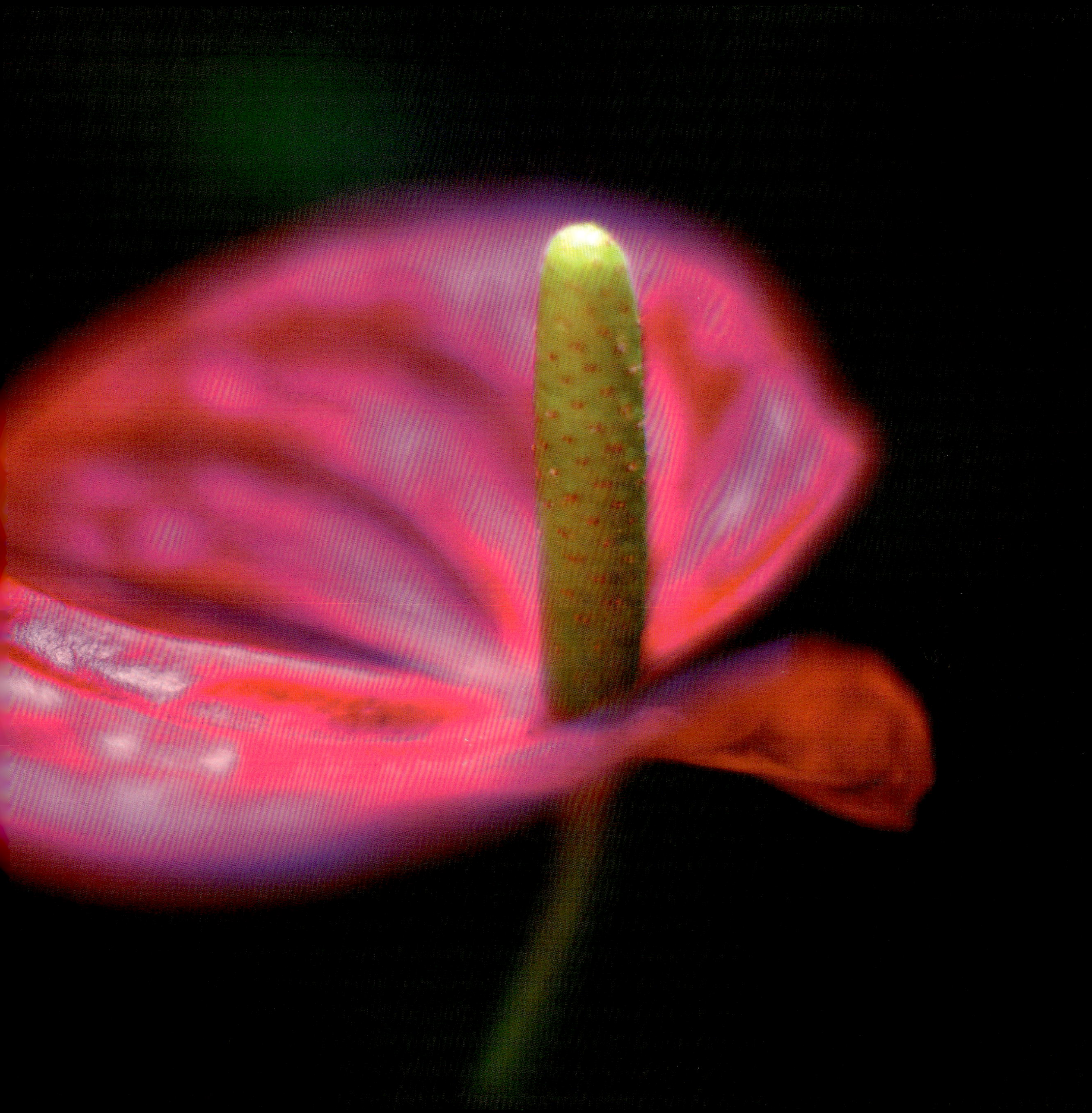

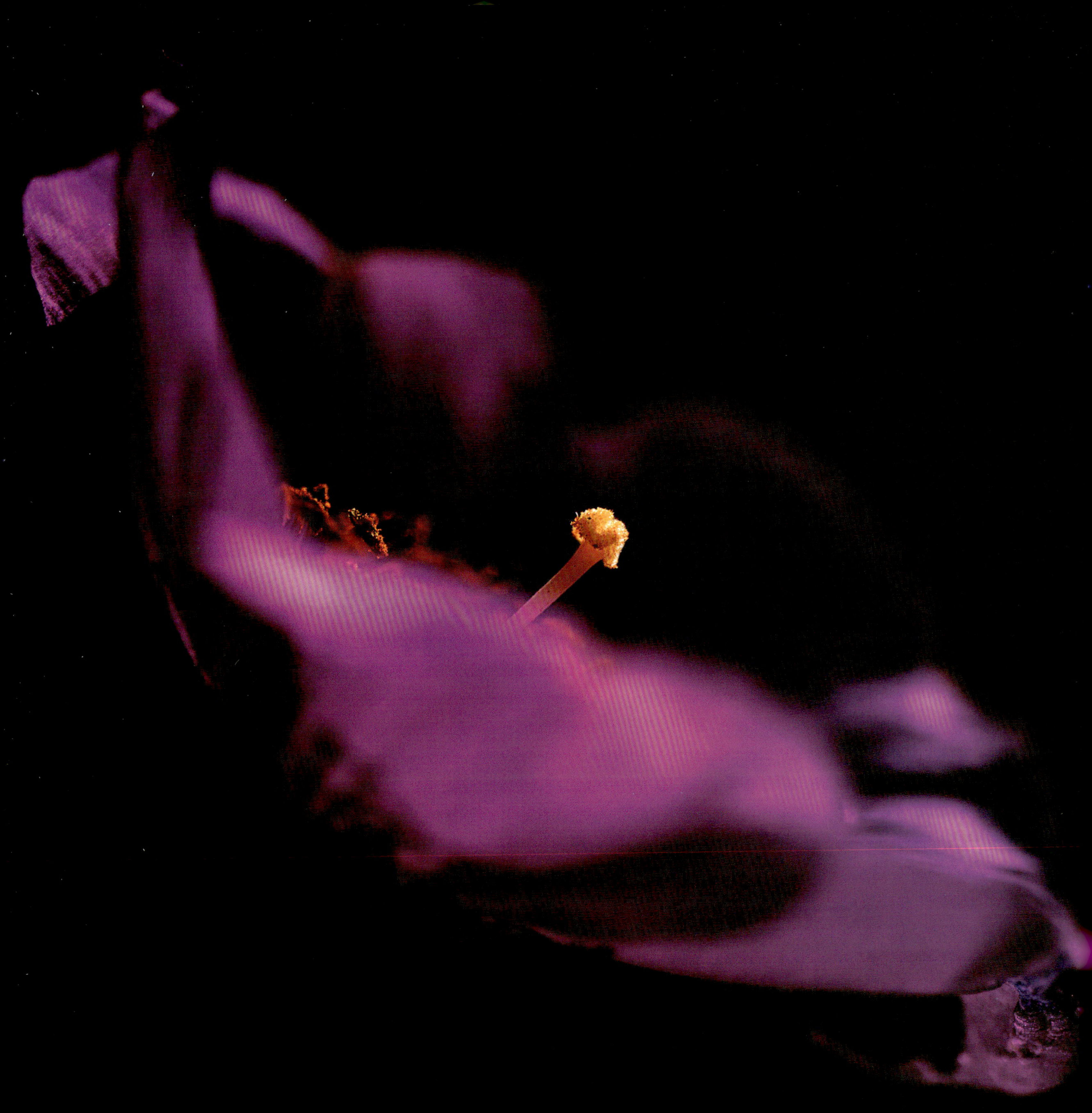

Rapturous, luscious, capricious
enticers of dreams, handmaidens of memories
sometime poisoners

Subjects of disciplined and undisciplined art

Flowers prove all things are possible

Wreathes for victors, solace for mourners
messengers of desire for the quivering

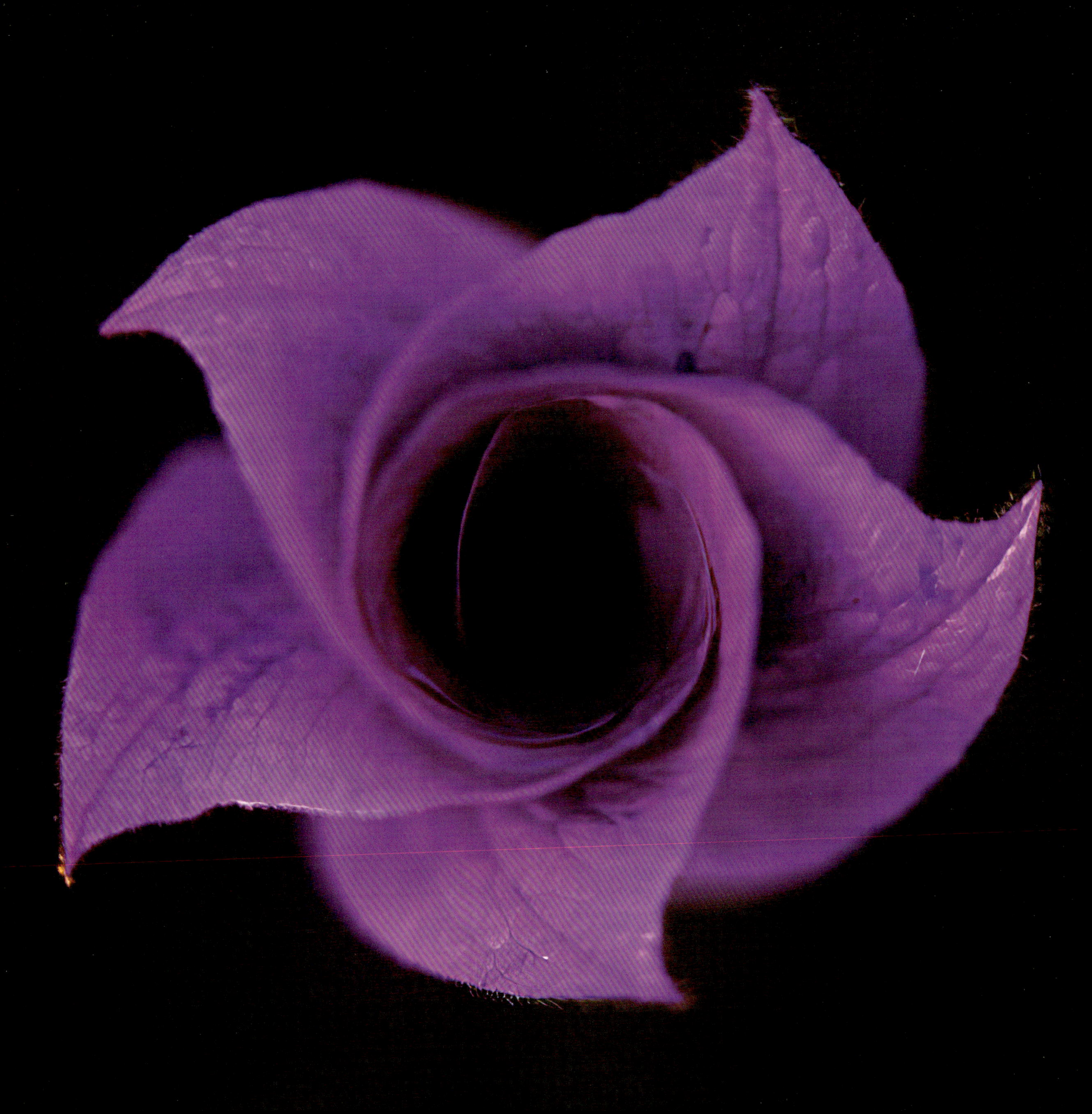

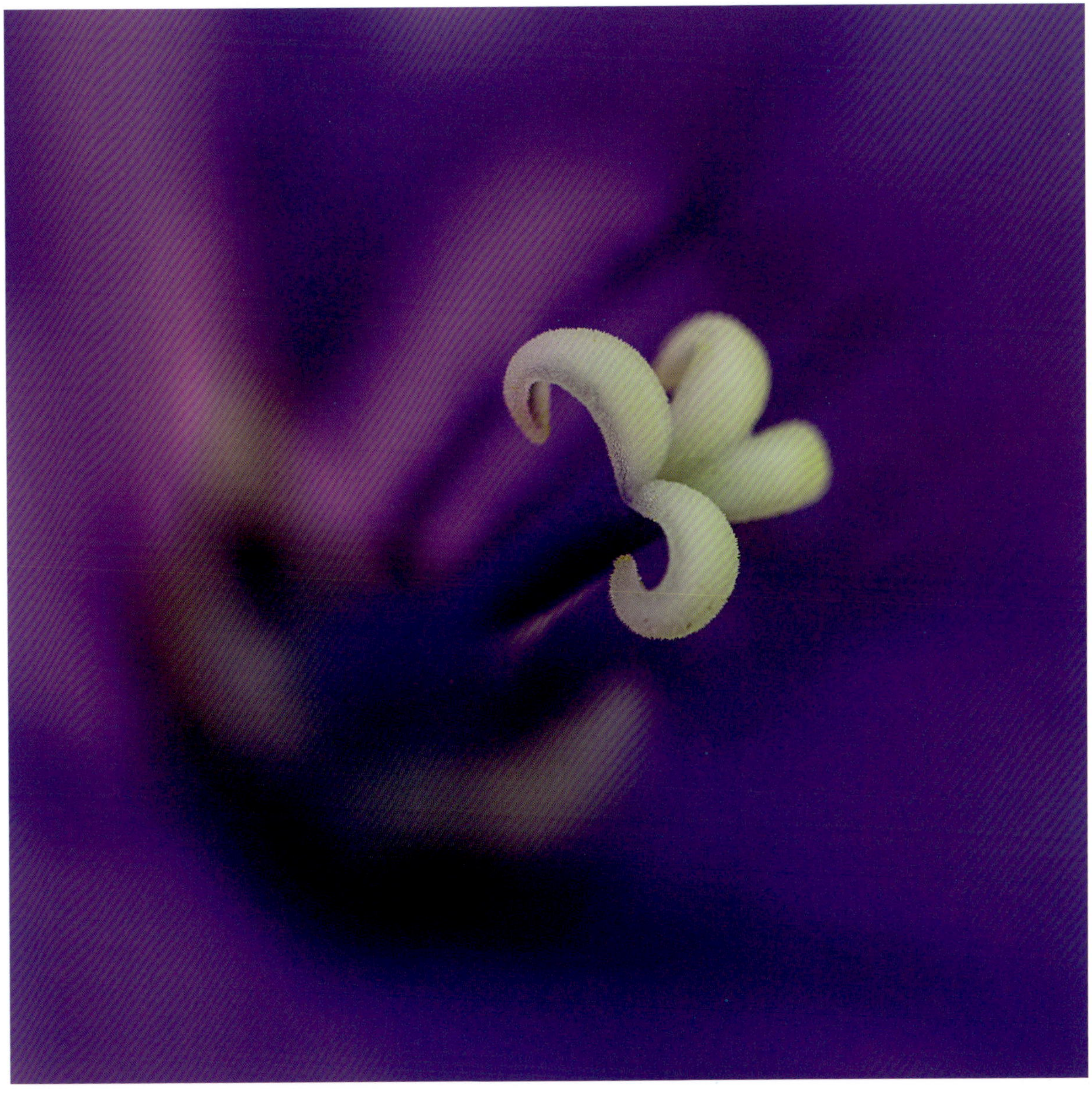

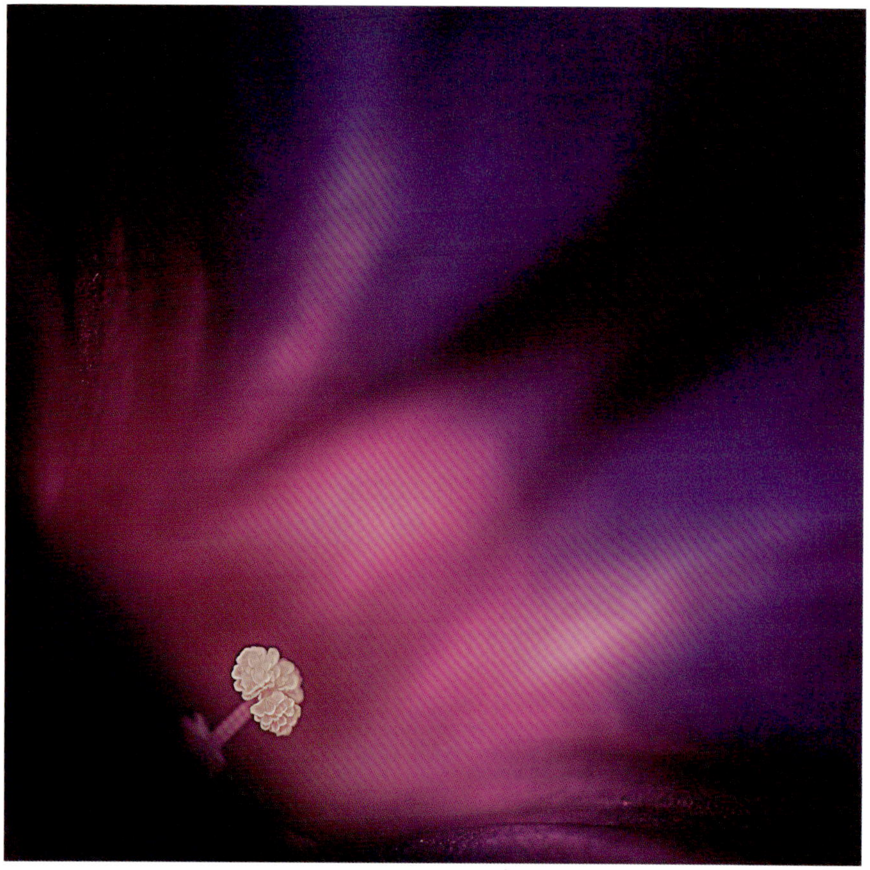

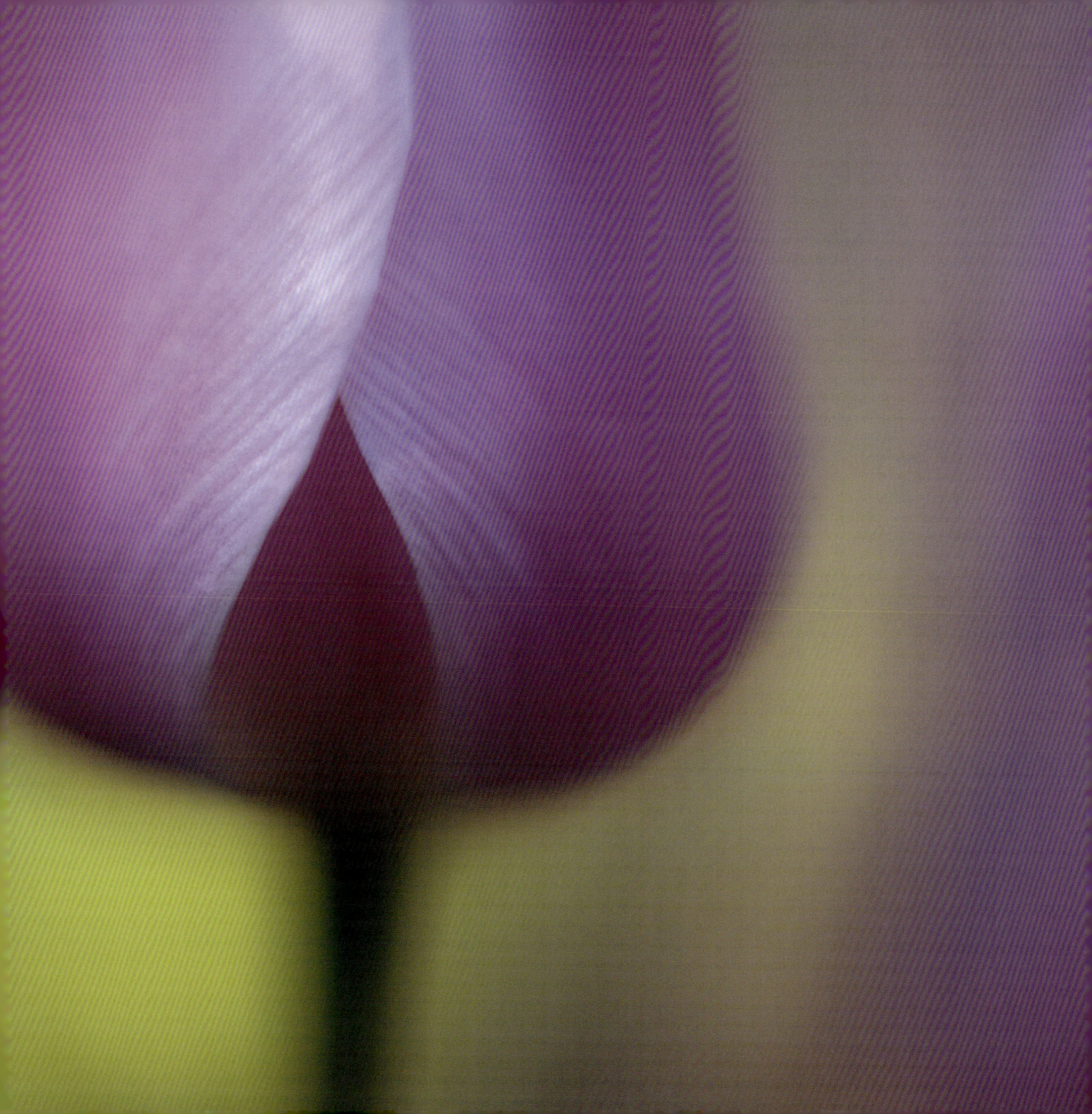

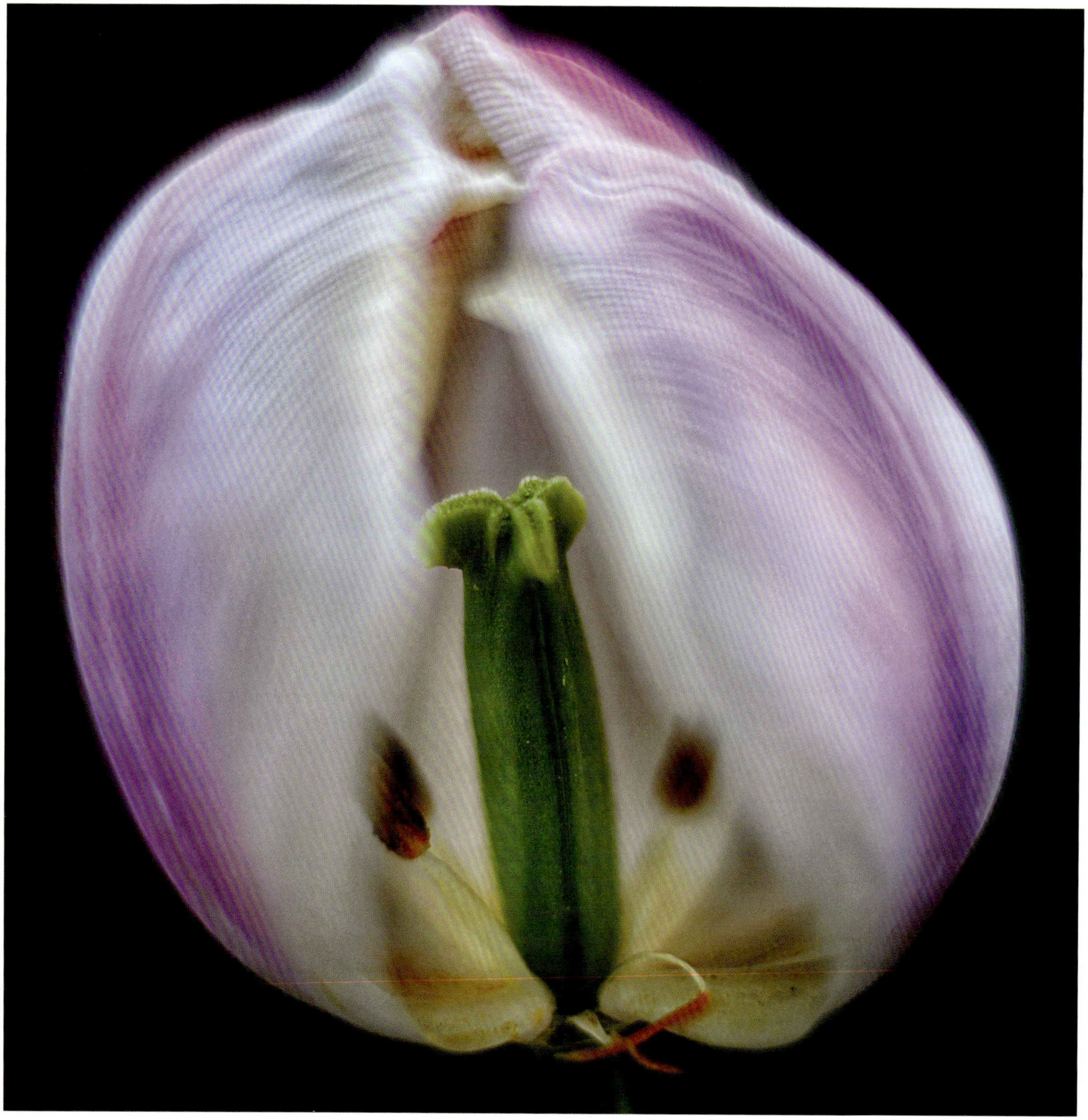

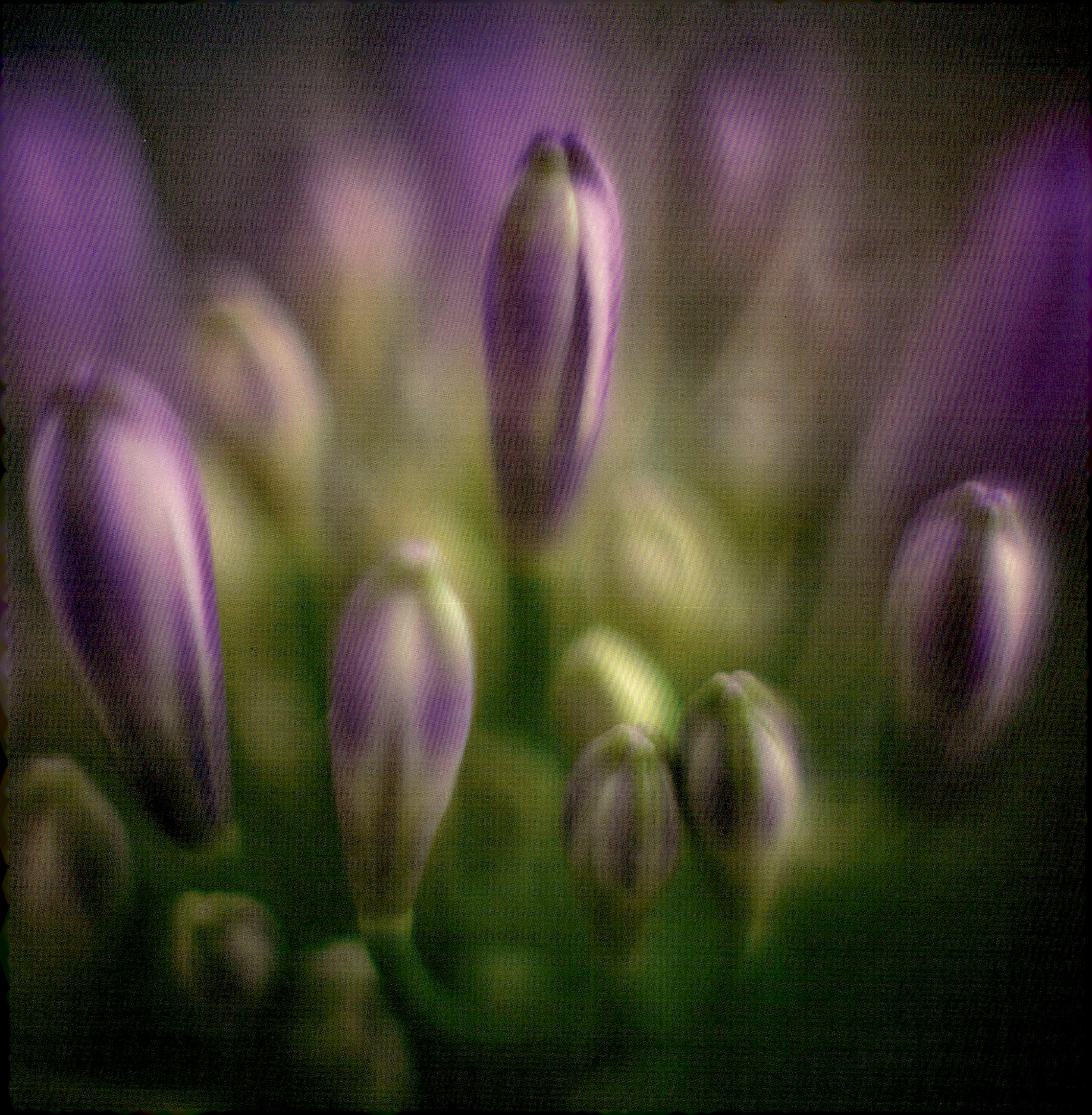

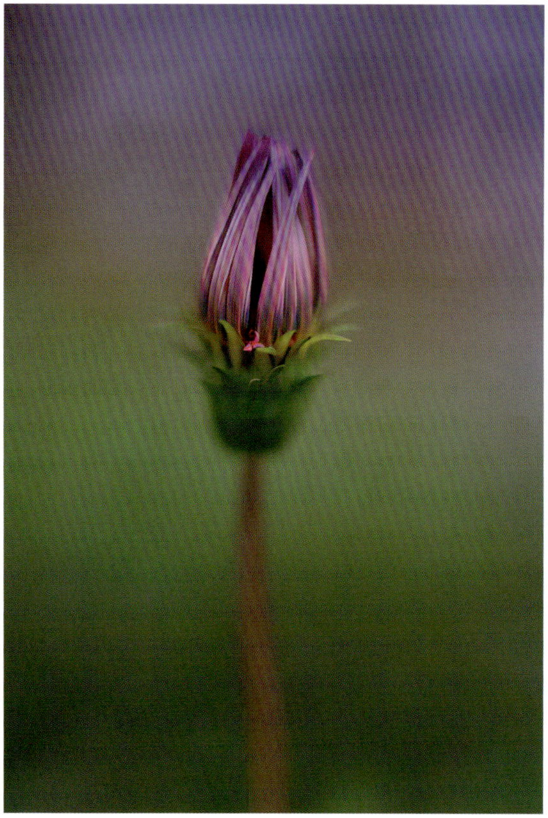

My petals of finest silk
will be shredded by circumstances
soiled by the rain that fed me
shriveled by the light that opened me.

To last a day or two—three!—is enough.

It is forever.

I will undress, gladly spent,
bowing to the rain and the sun.

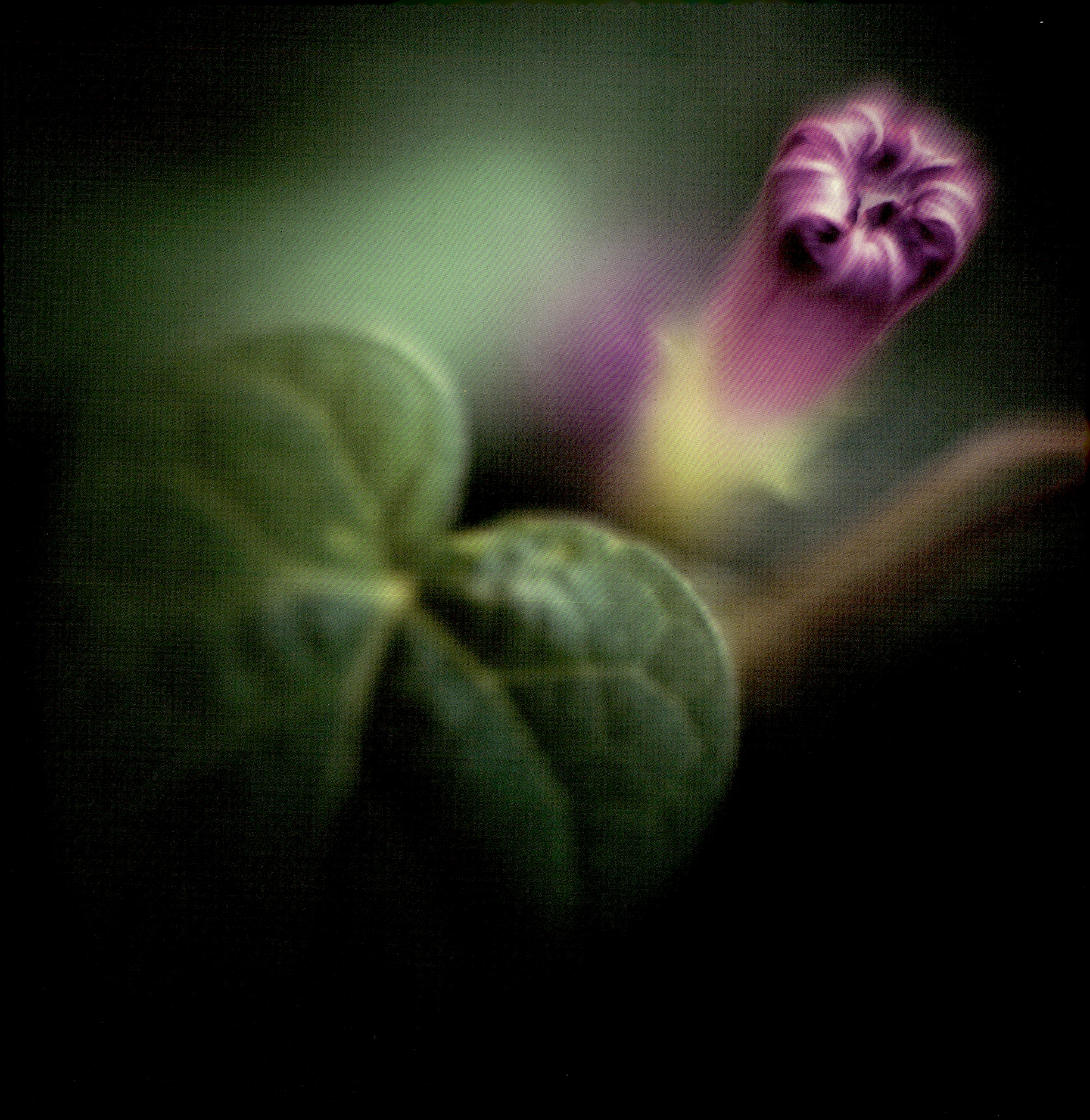

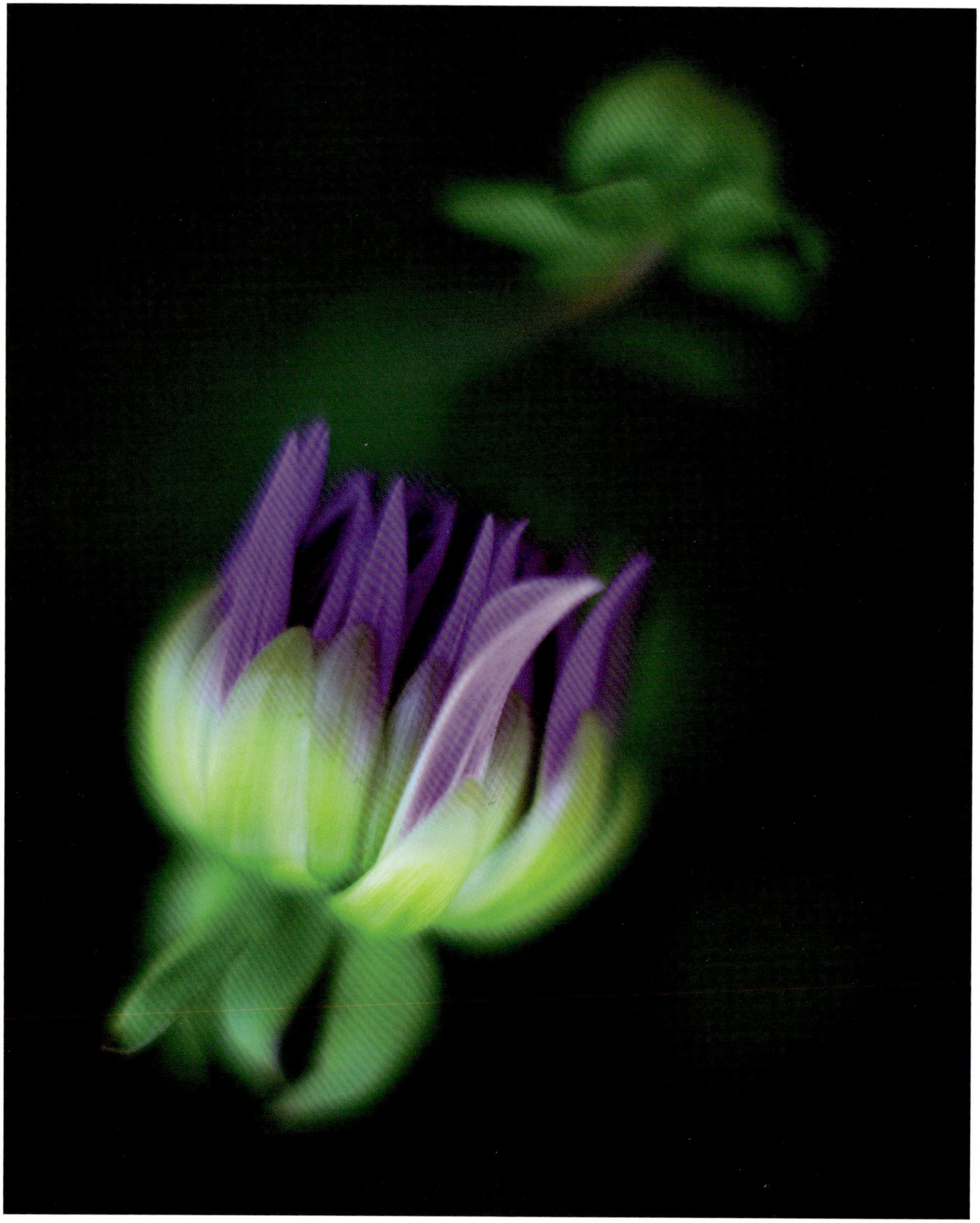

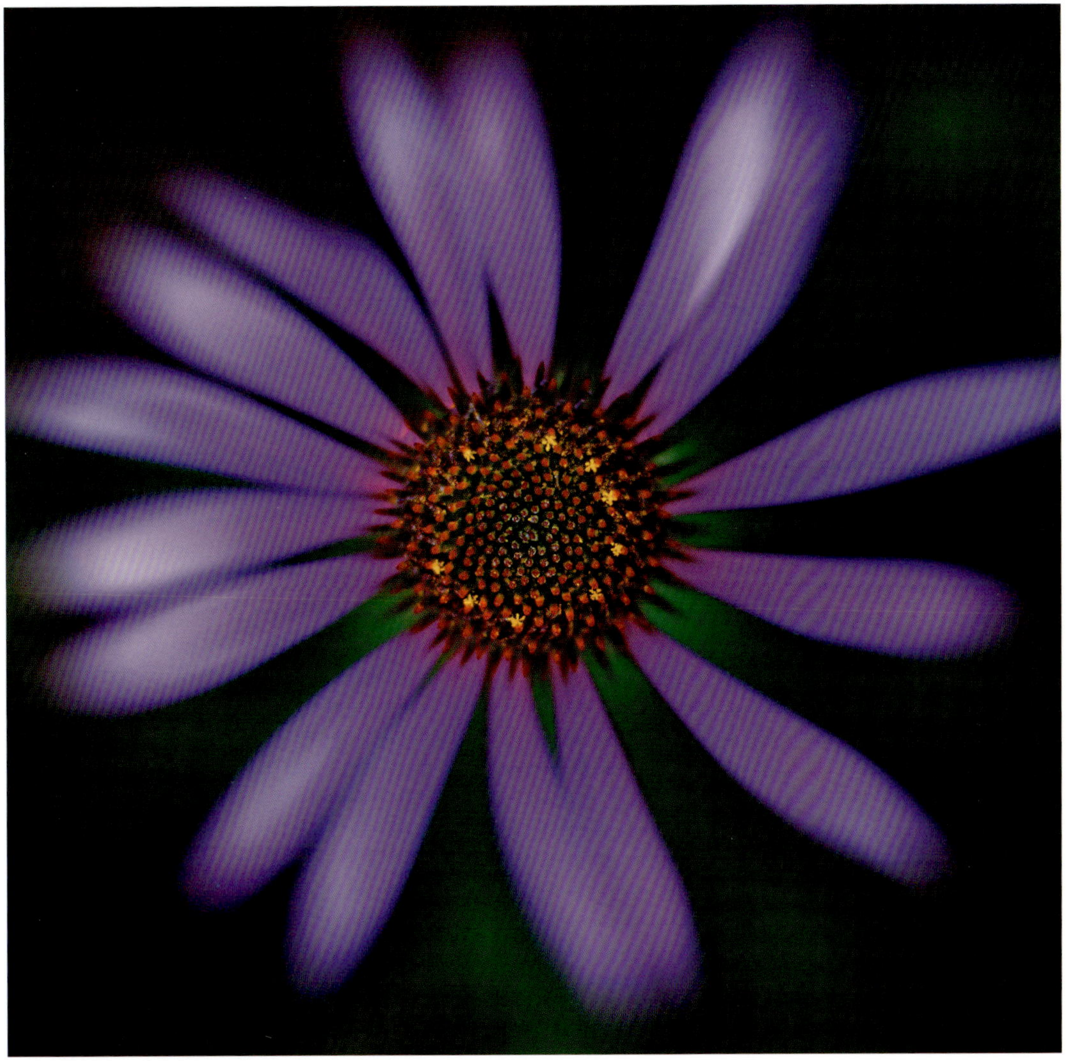

Why fret about
the nature of God
when flowers show
the beneficence of nature?

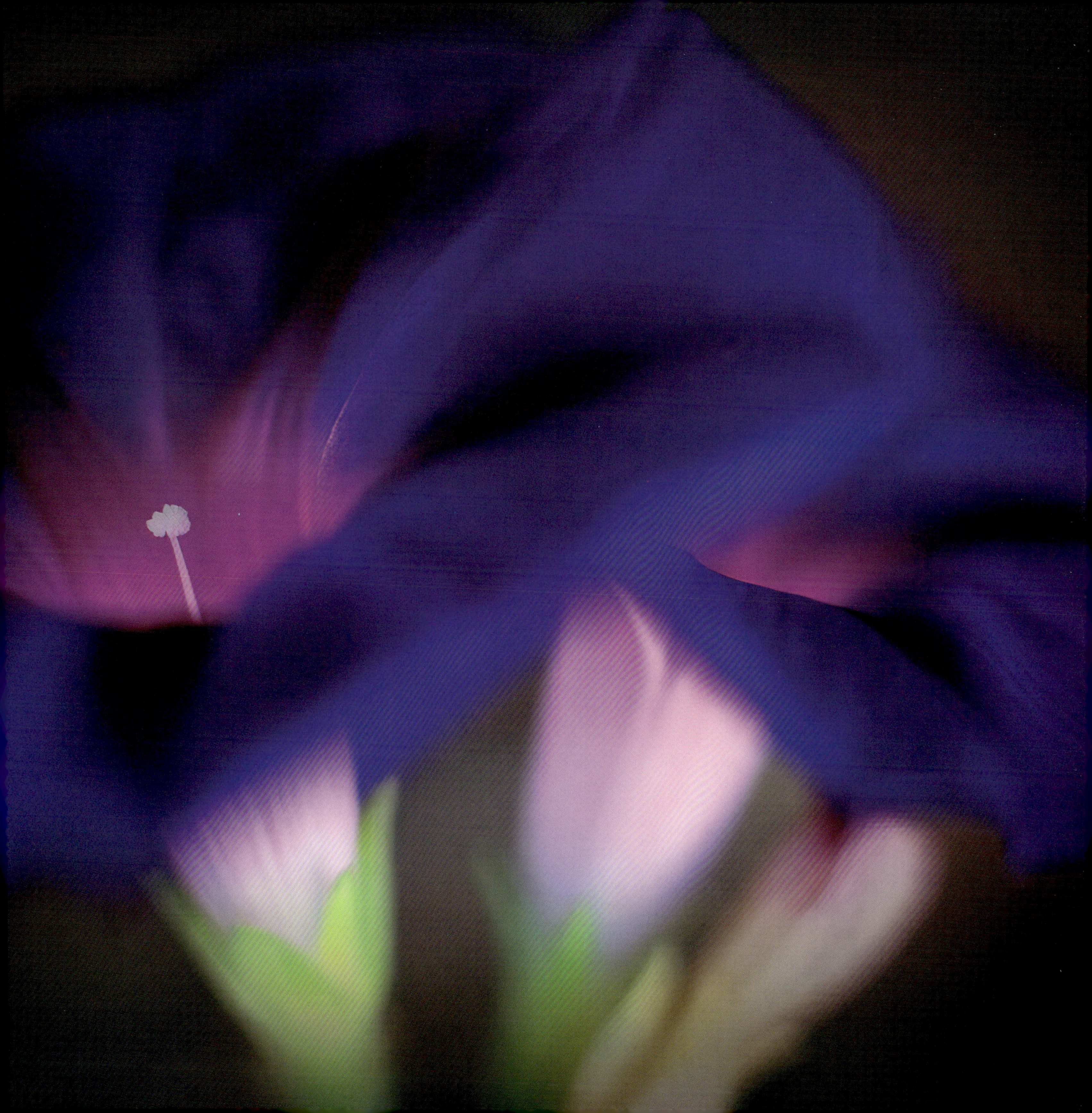

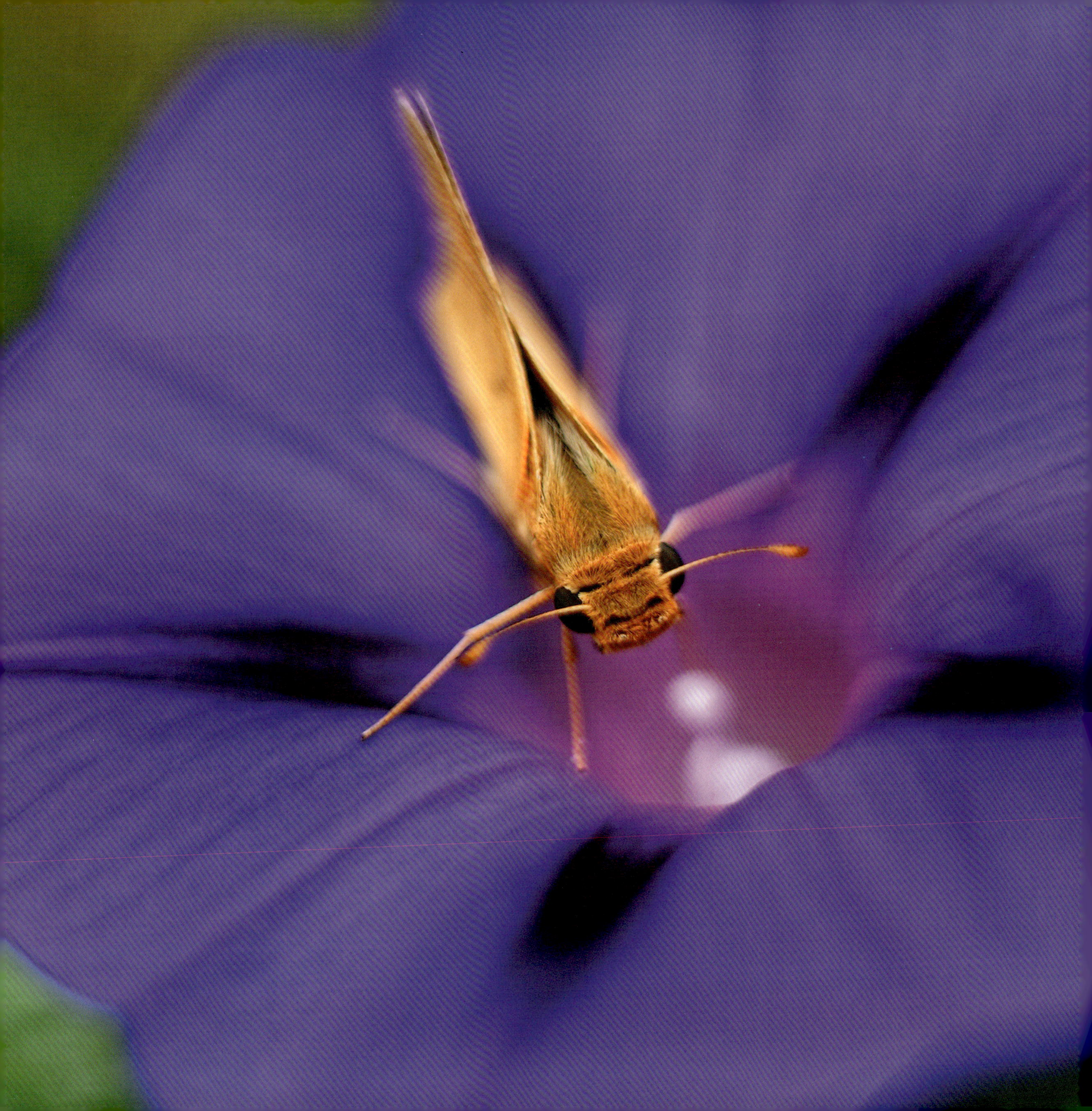

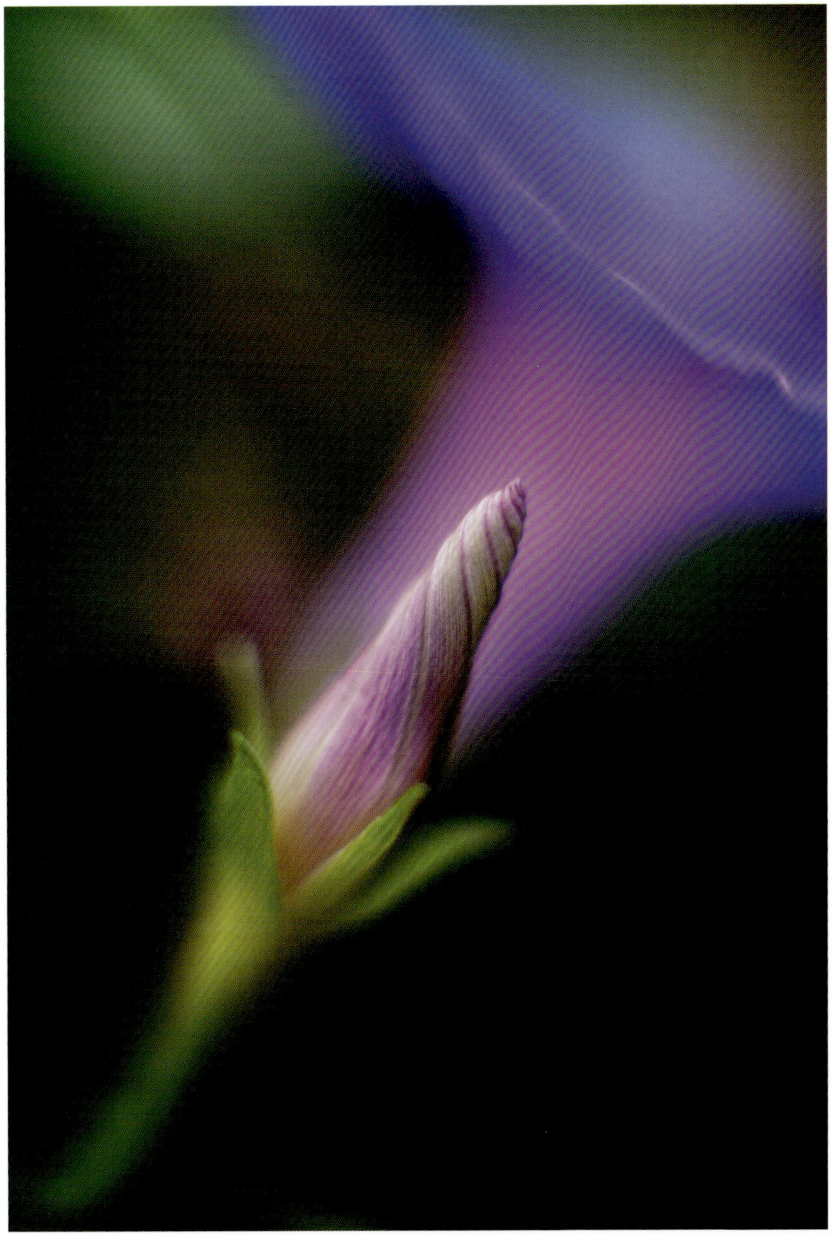

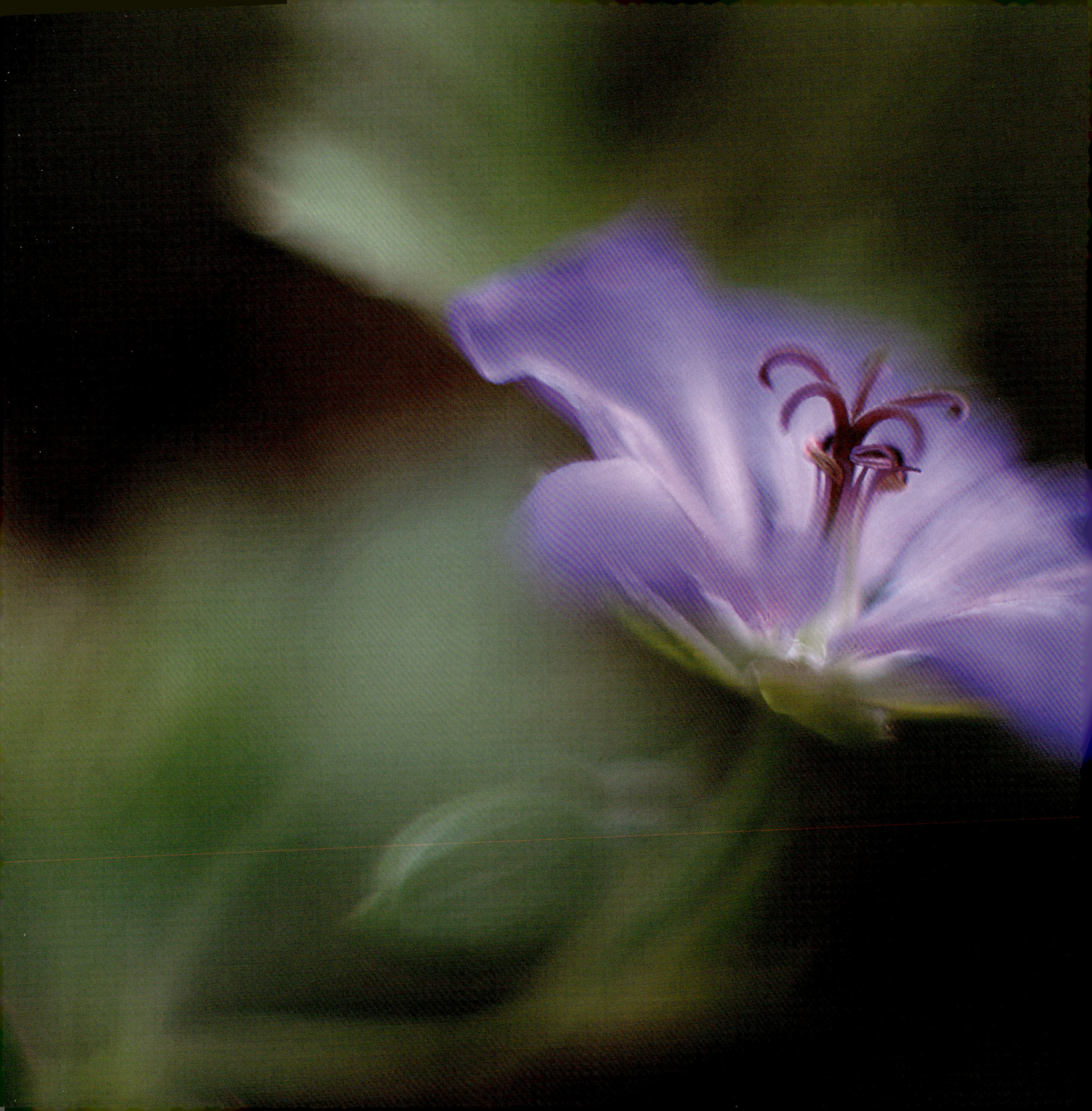

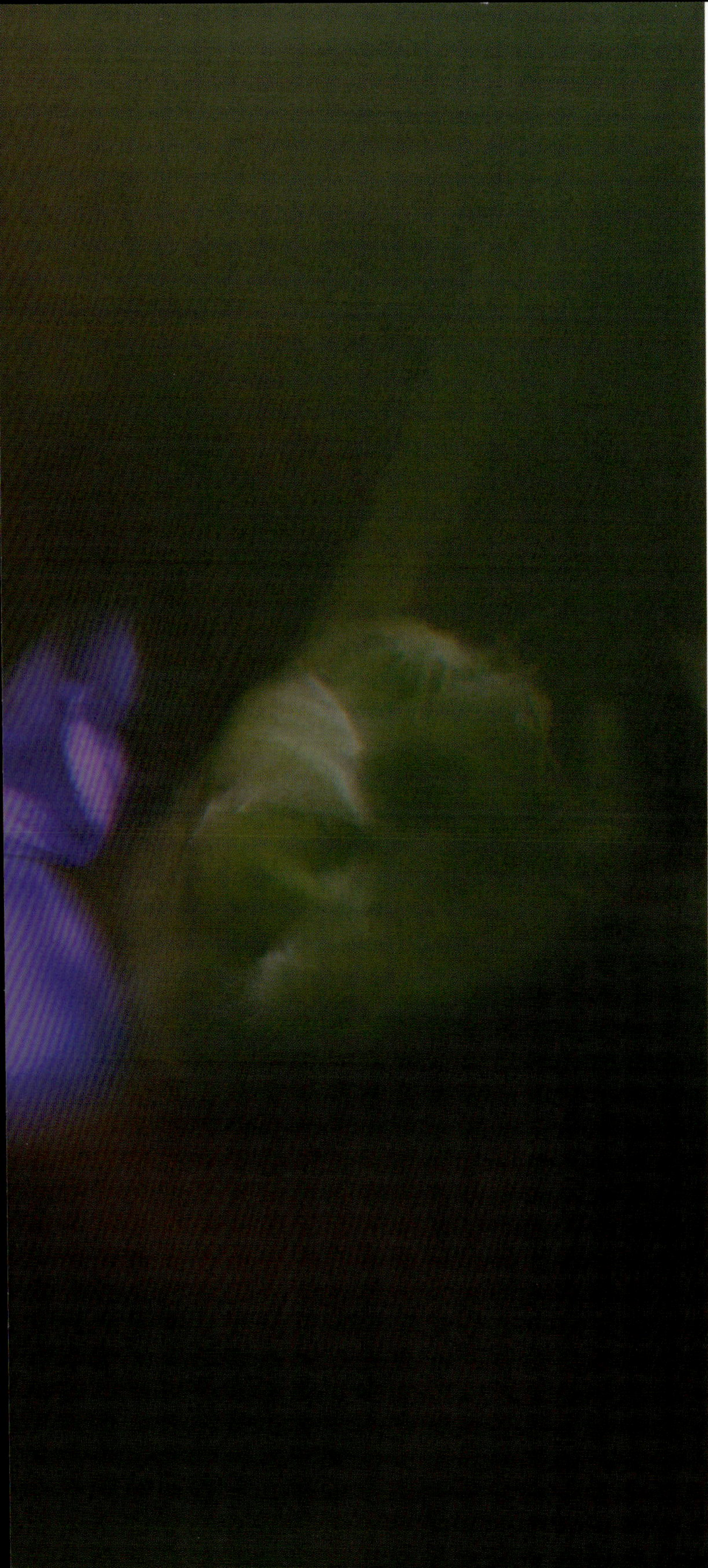

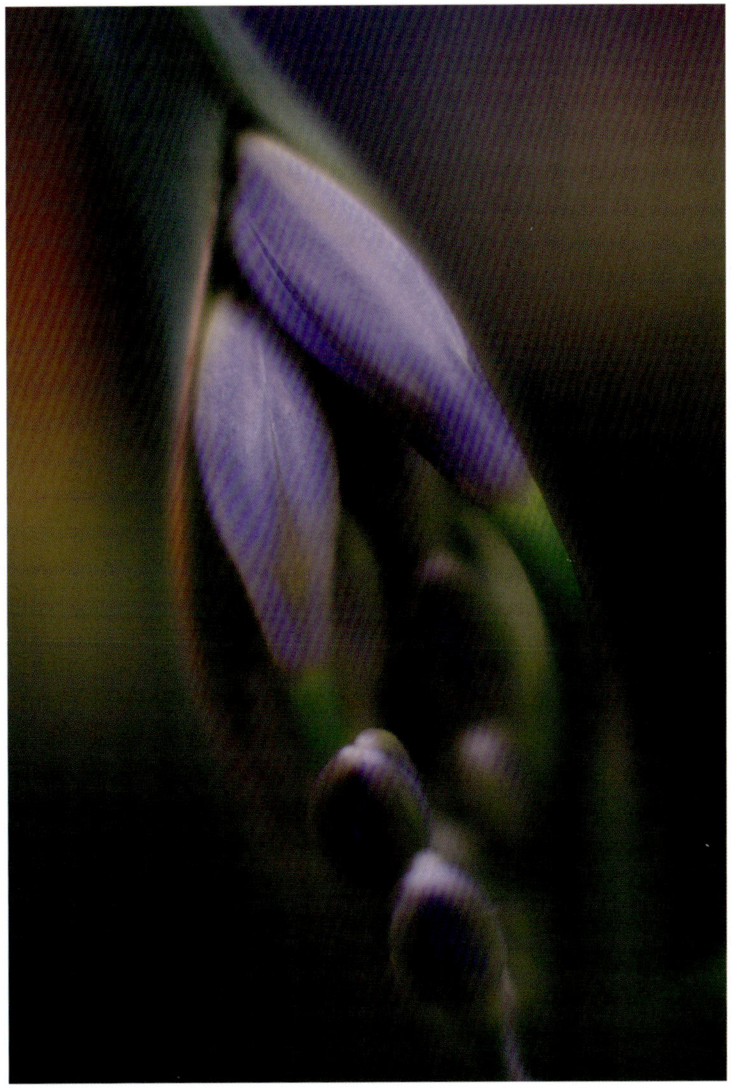

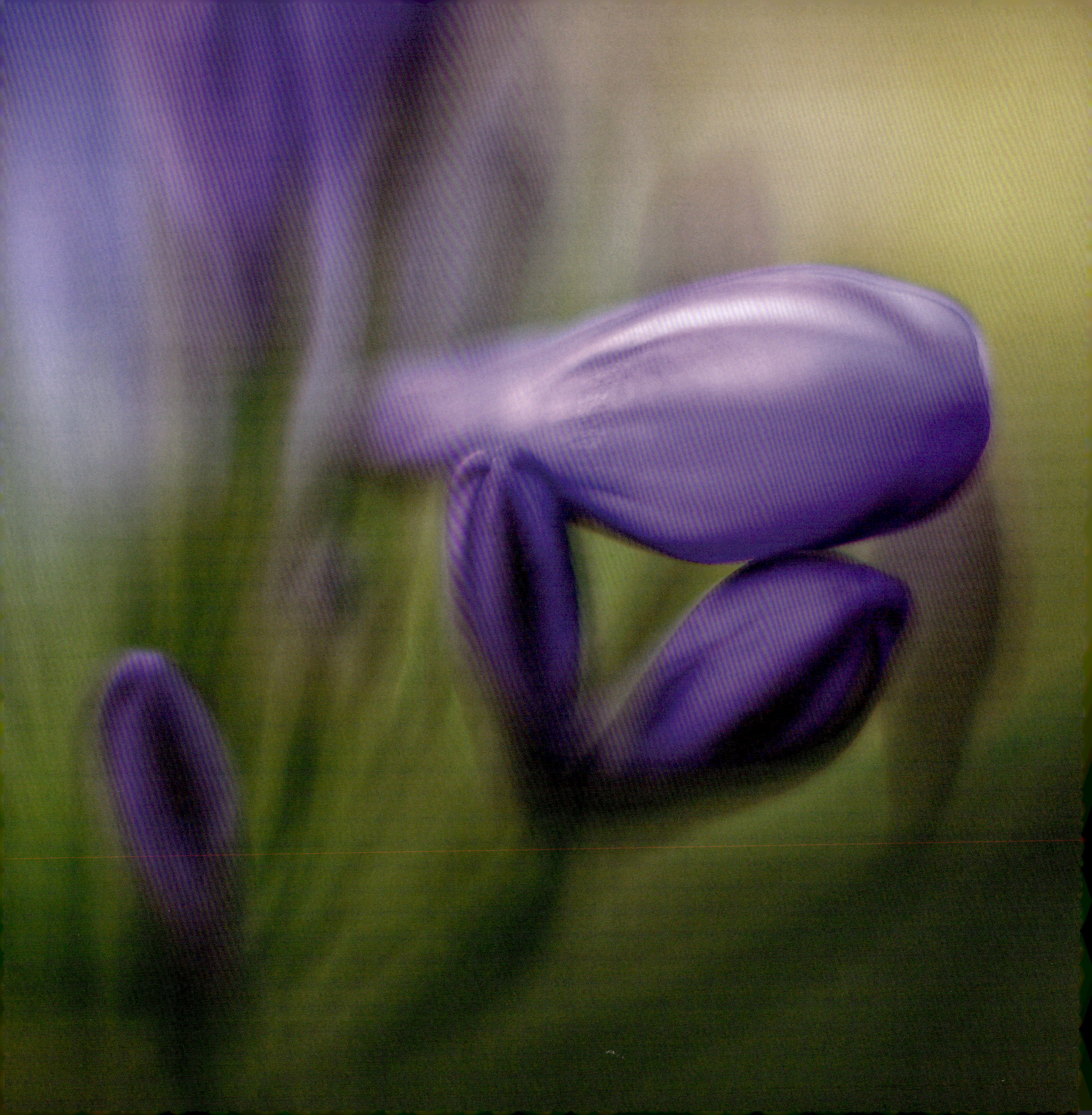

Purple, child of trysts
between imperious red and lonely blue

fire and water

worn by flowers and emperors
strutting grandeur and wielding scepters
in ancient Rome, Egypt, Persia,
and backyards.

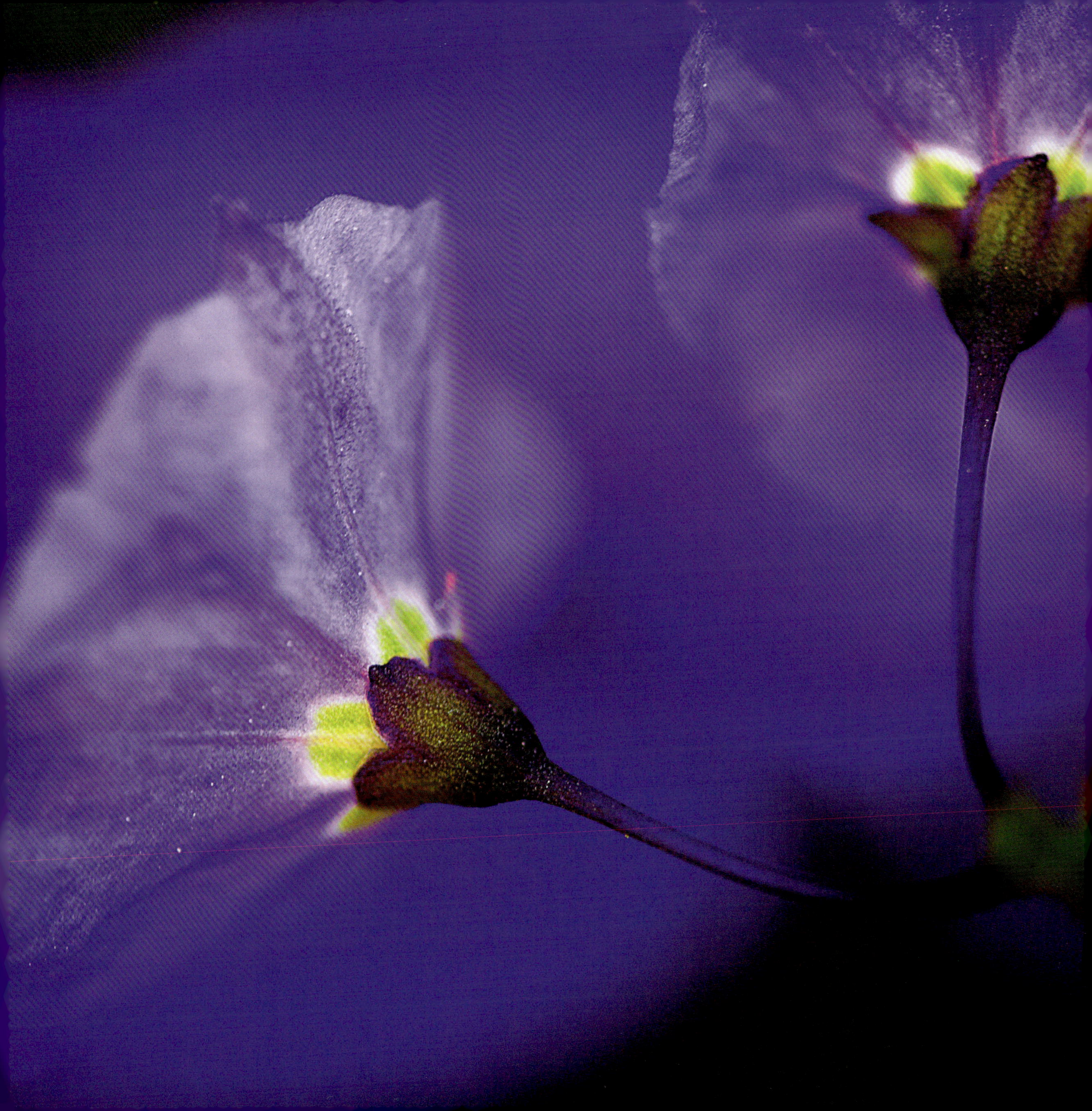

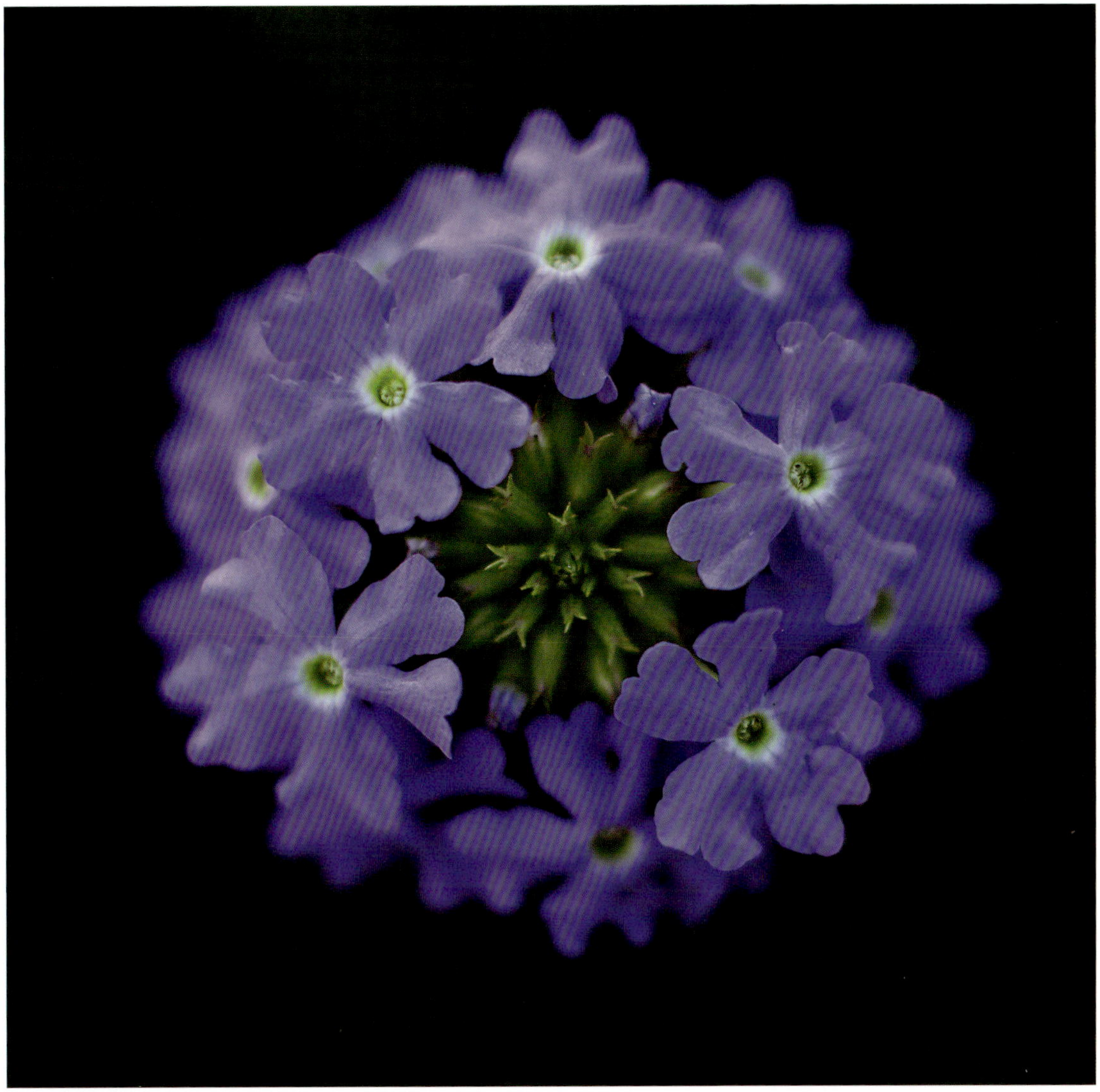

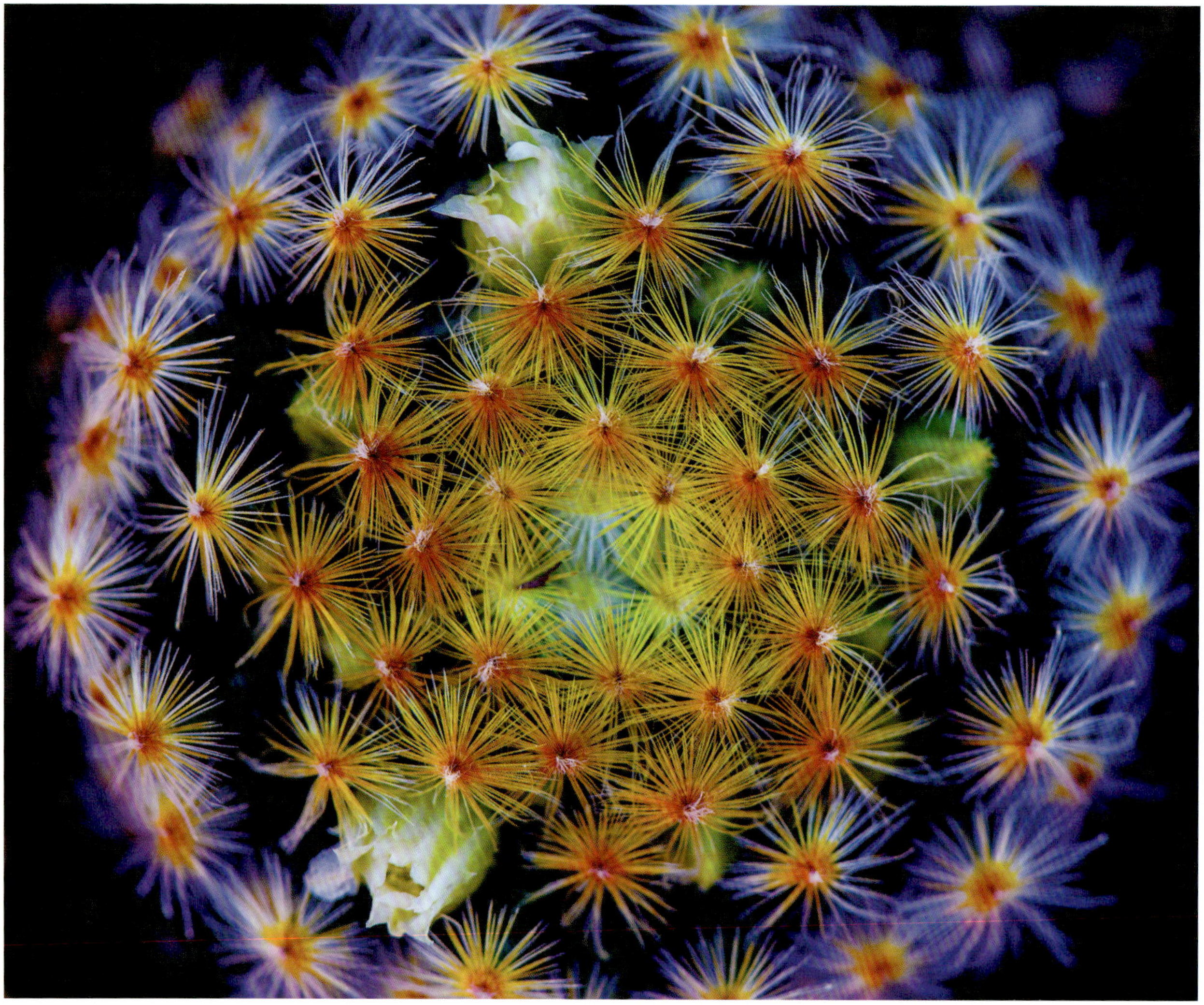

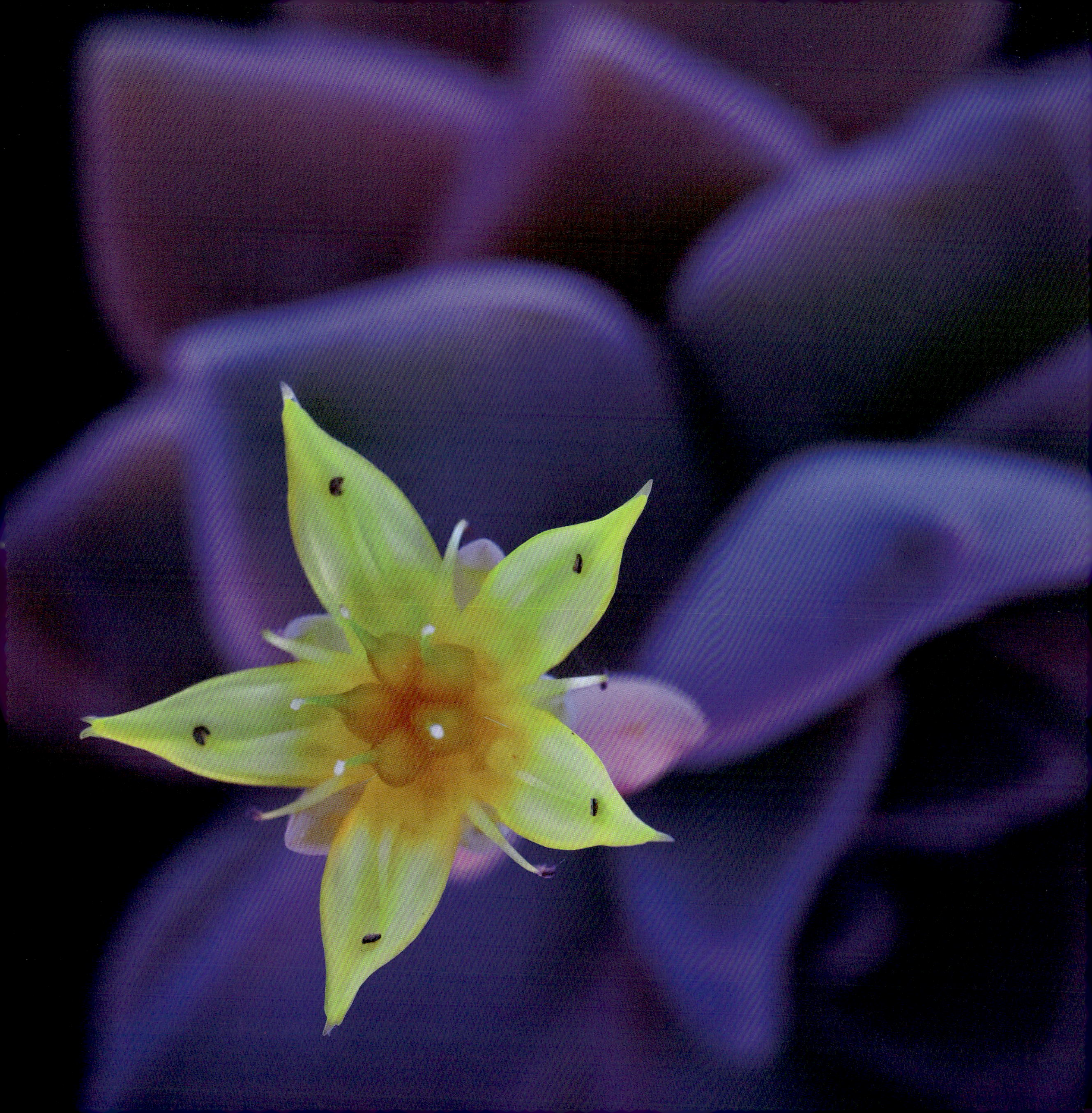

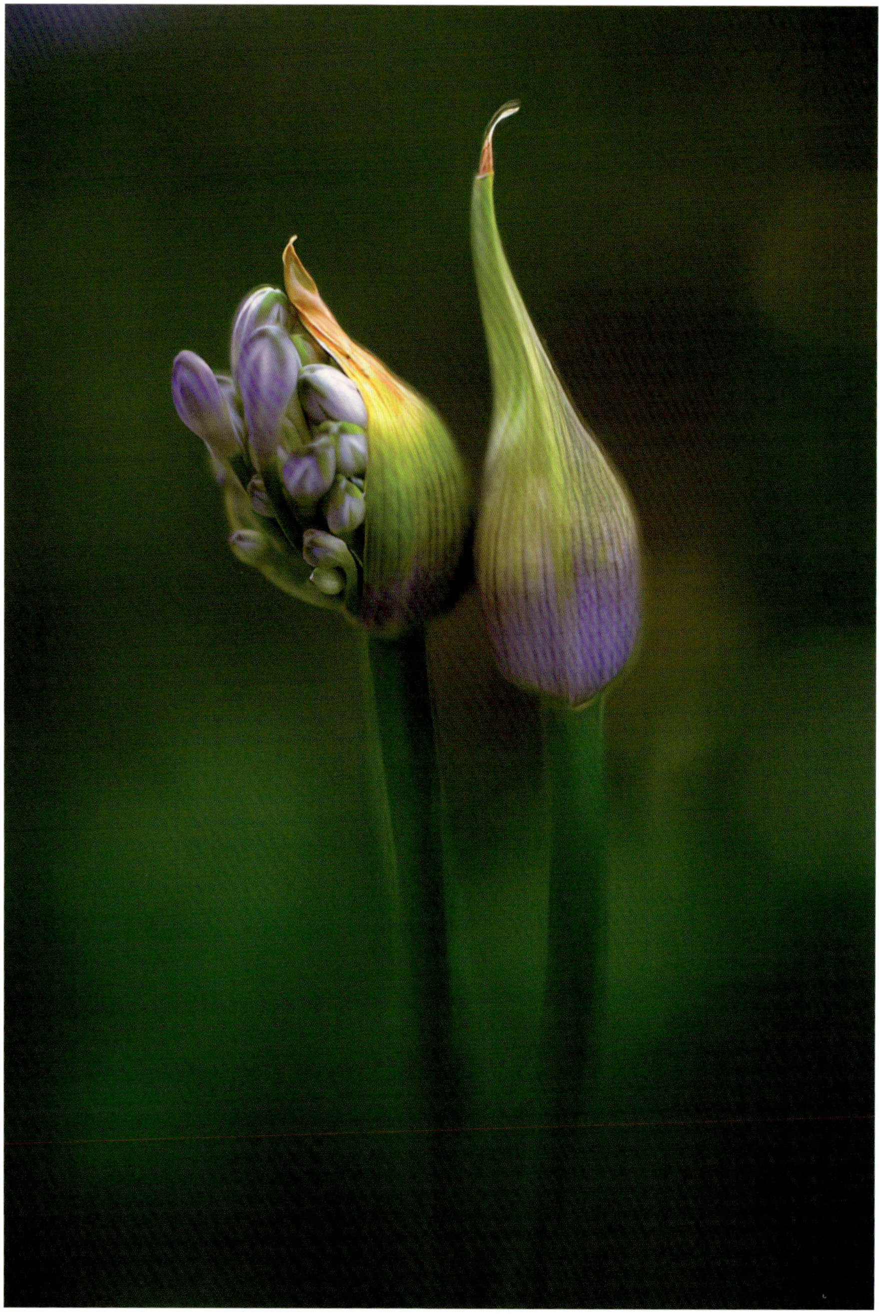

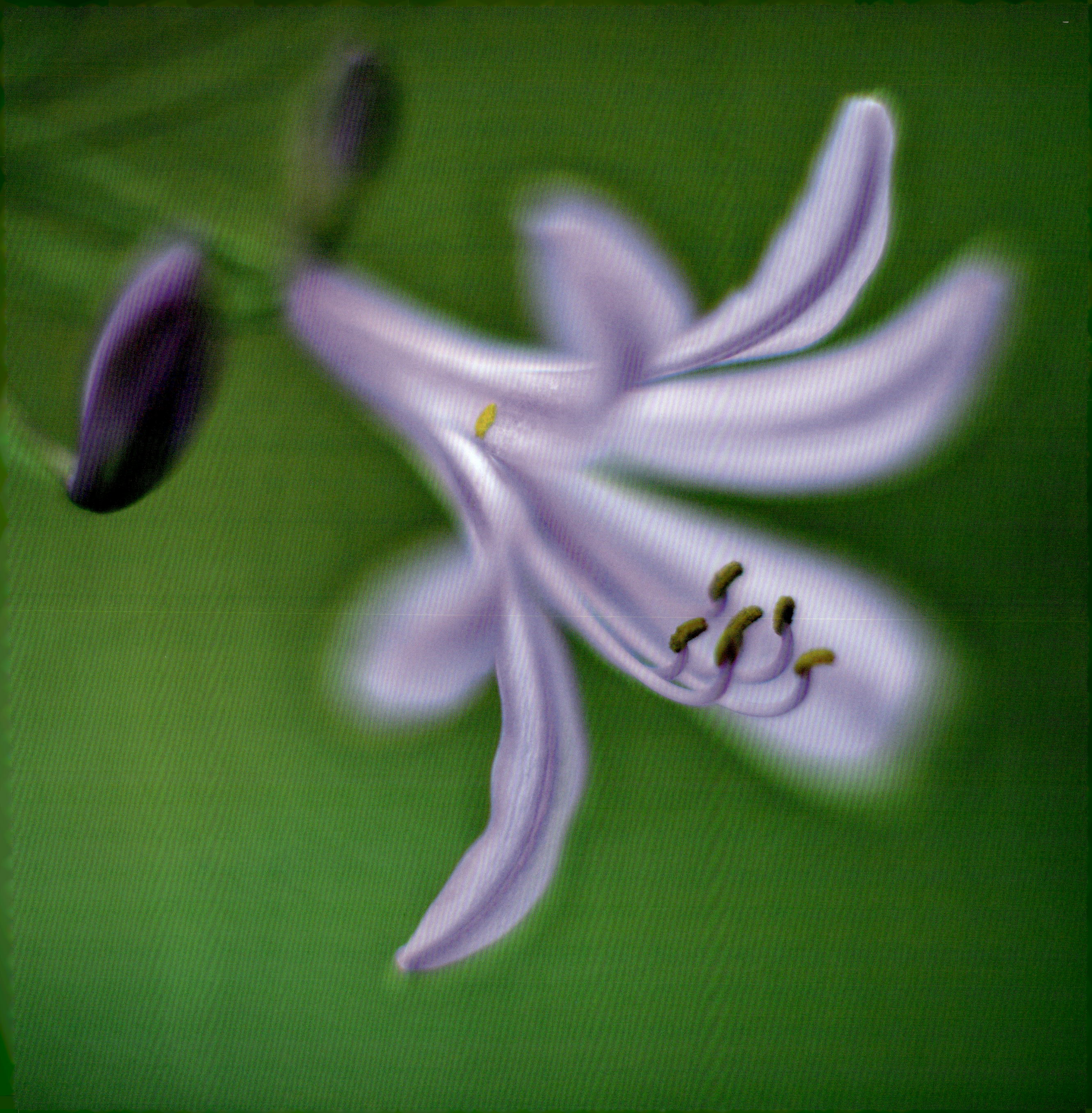

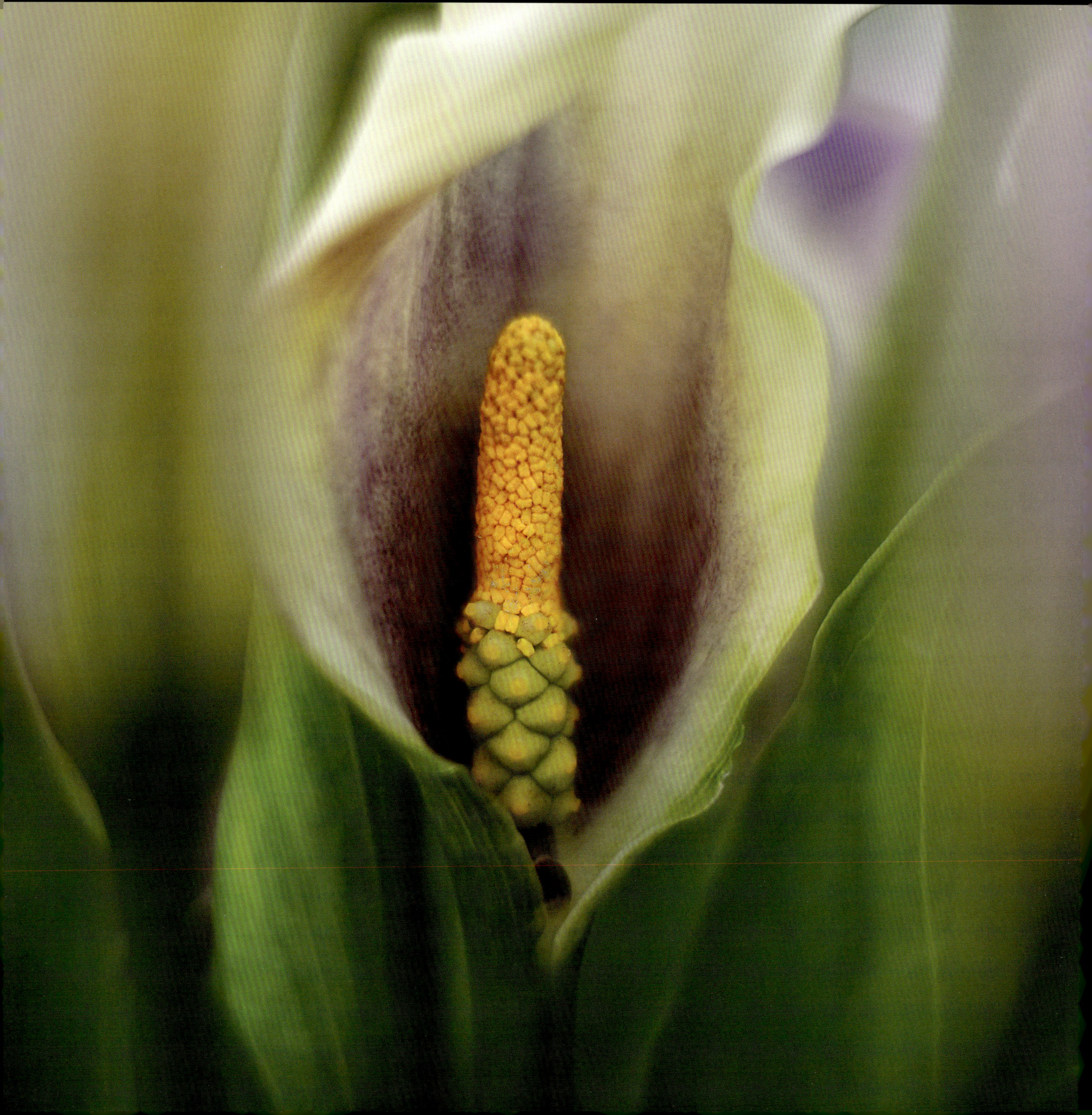

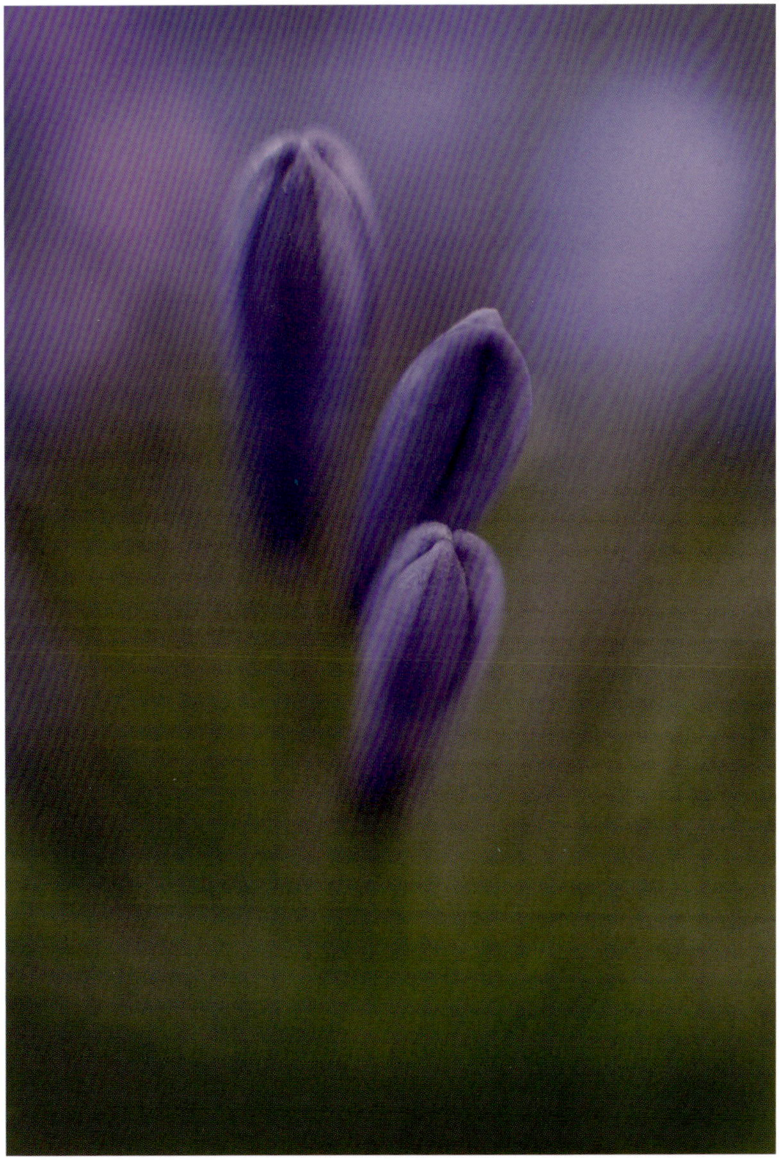

cerulean, Delft, kingfisher
cyan, globe thistle, gentian
hydrangea, peacock
periwinkle, cobalt
navy, blue heron

midnight, delphinium
fountain blue lobelia
blue racer constrictor
Crayola, Caribbean

blue dasher dragonfly
indigo, lazuli
Prussian, sky
morpho butterfly

azure, forget-me-not
salvia, sapphire
cornflower, Klein
lowdown dirty dog
morning glory, aqua

baby blues
blueberry, blue balls
blue bells, blue jay
blue blood, blue moon
blue-footed booby
blue-bottom baboon
robin's egg

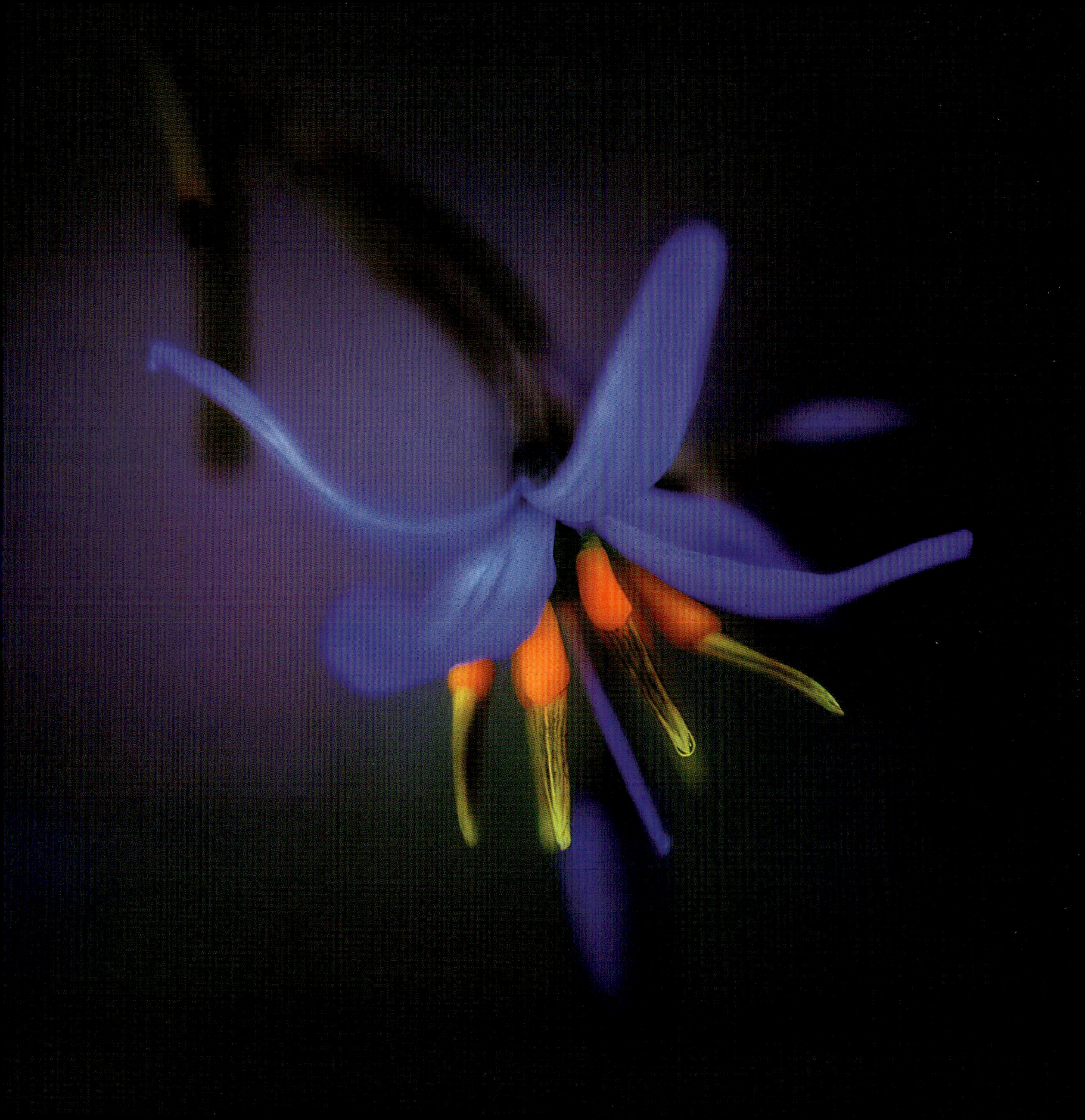

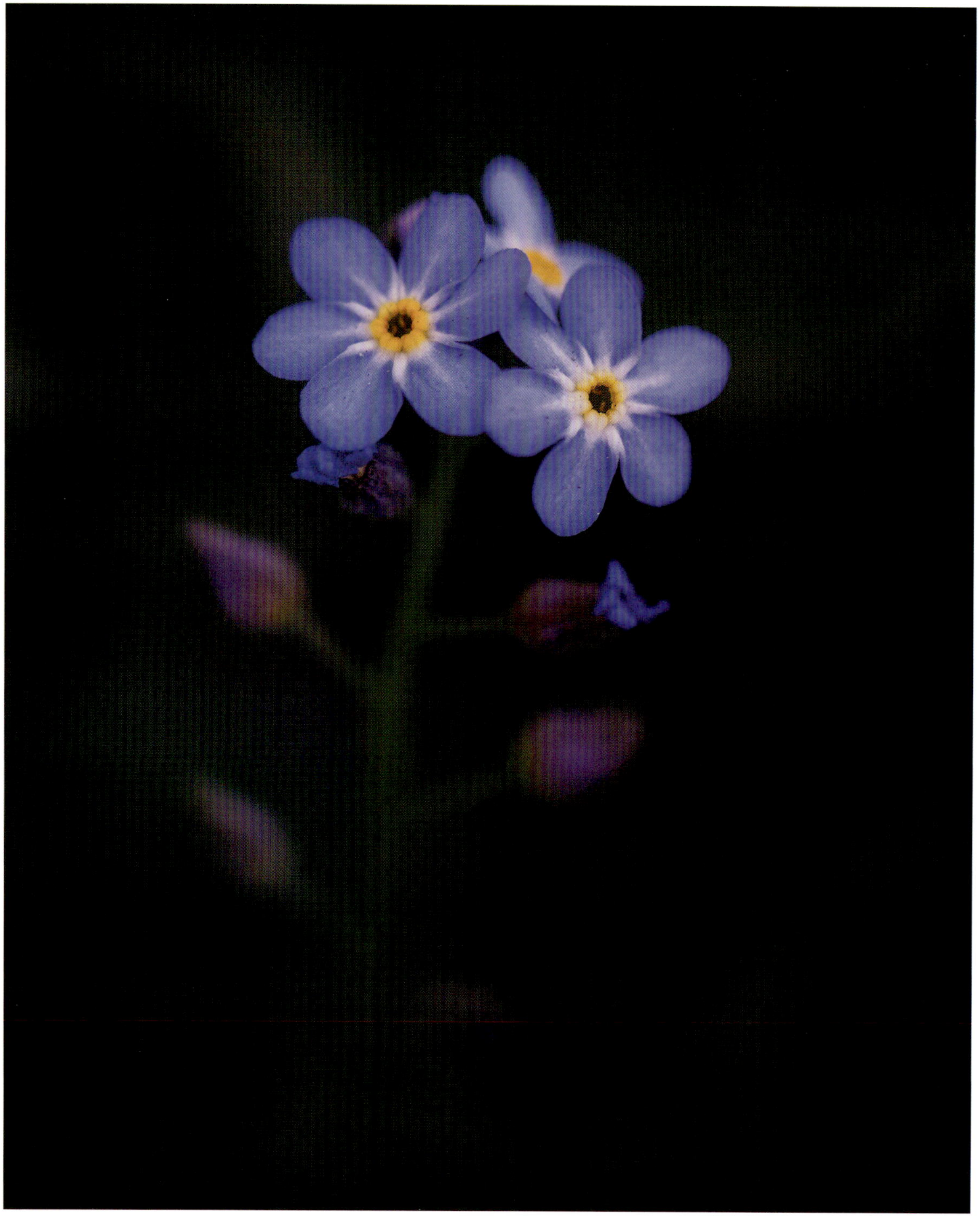

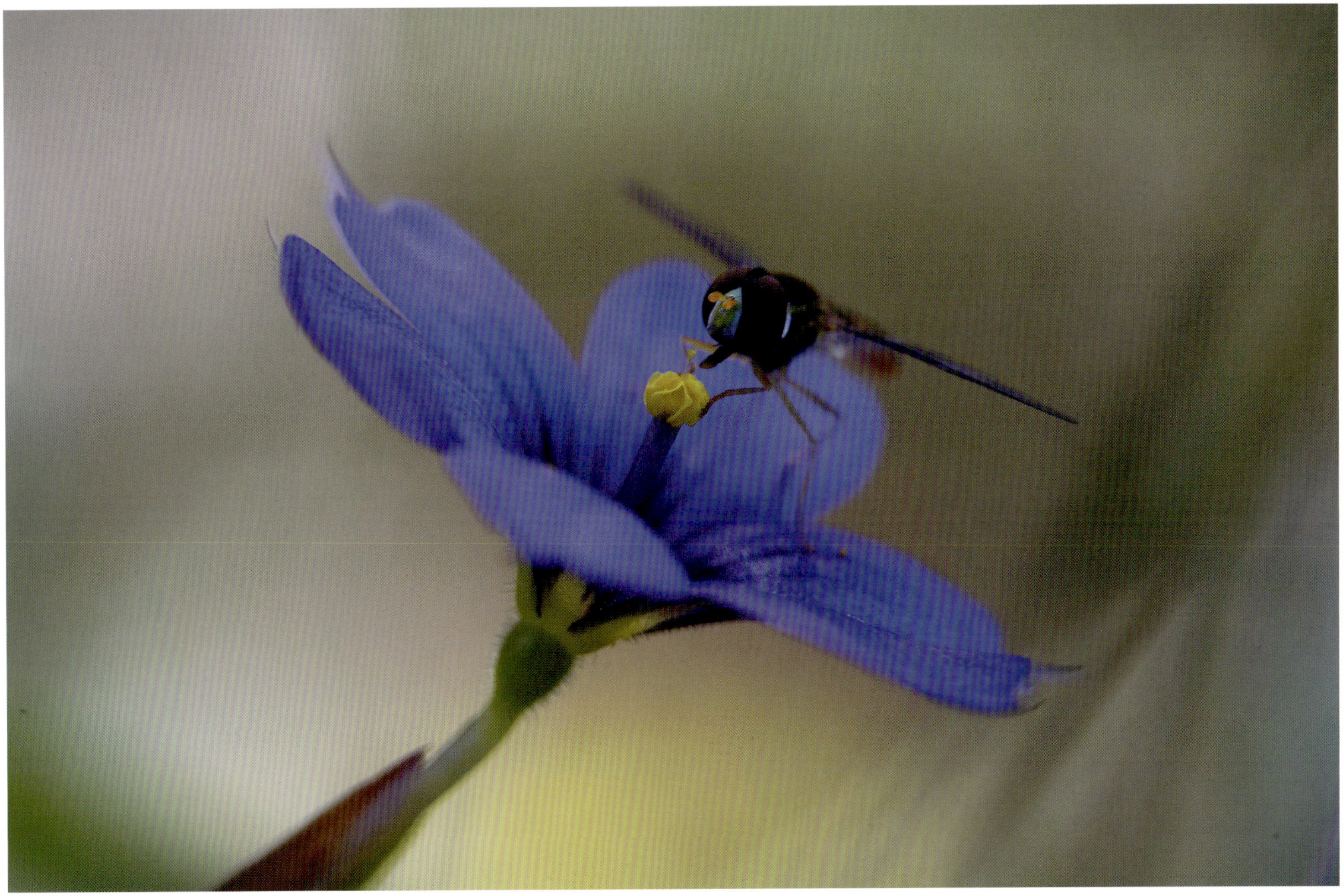

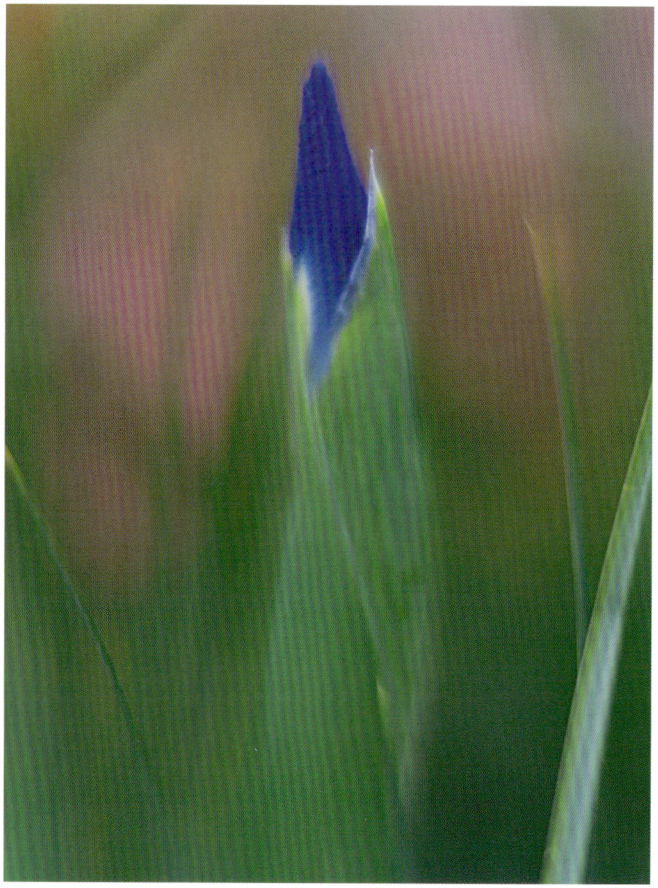

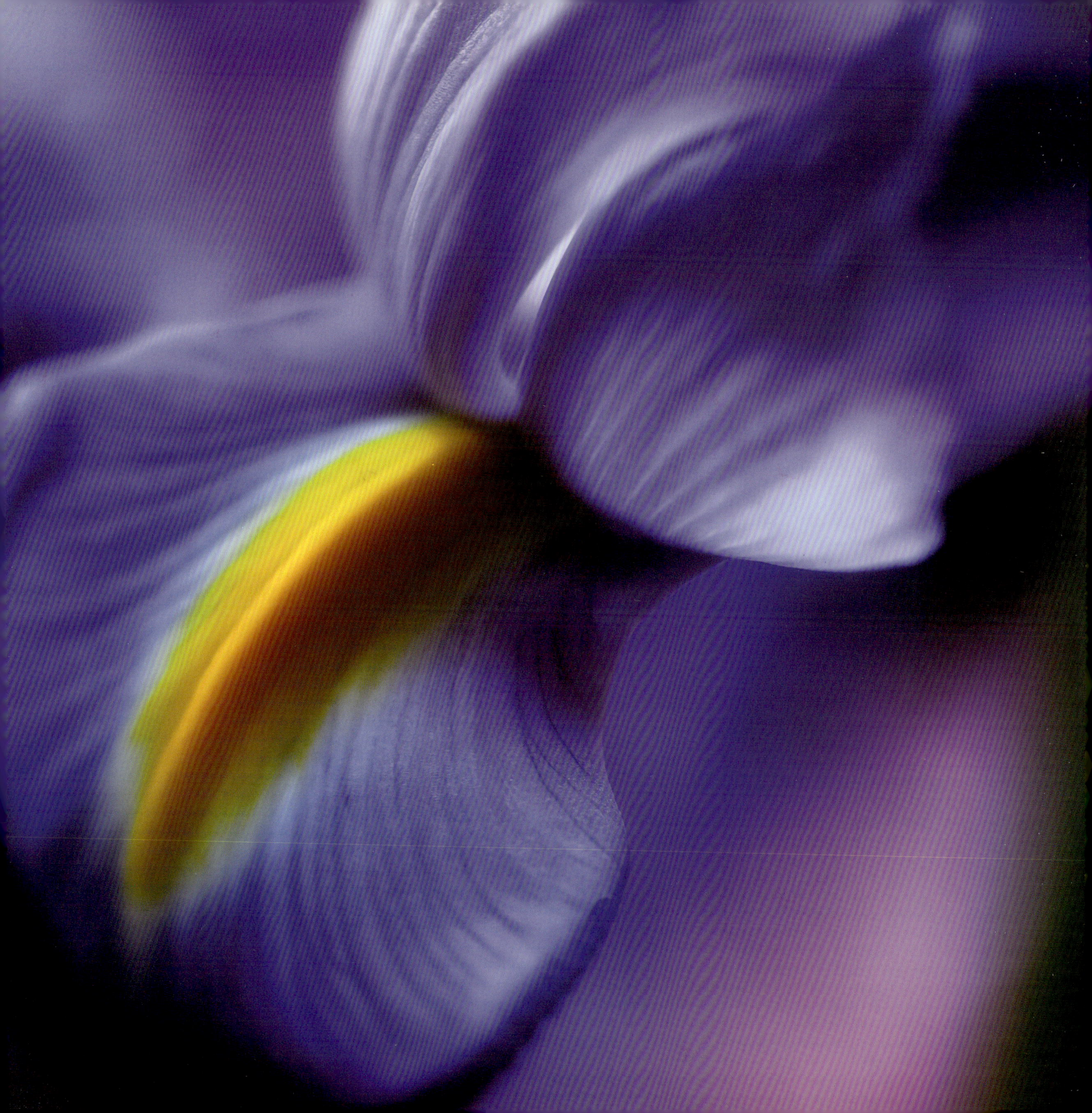

BOTANICAL & COMMON NAMES

PROVIDED BY AARON LANDWORTH

GARDEN CONCIERGE

FRONT COVER: *Anagallis arvensis.* Pimpernel

BACK COVER: *Papaver nudicaule,* Icelandic poppy

Pg 9, 10: *Papaver nudicaule,* Icelandic poppy

Pg 13: *Zinnia elegans*, Zinnia

Pg 15: *Asclepias curassavica* seeds, Monarch Milkweed/Tropical Milkweed

Pg 16: *Agapanthus africanus,* Peter Pan White/ Dwarf White Lily of the Nile

Pg 19: *Agapanthus africanus,* Albus/White Lily of the Nile

Pg 22-26: *Zantedeschia*, Calla Lily

Pg 29: *Gazania*, African Daisy

Pg 30, 31: *Tulipa,* Tulip

Pg 32: *Zantedeschia*, Calla Lily

Pg 33: *Echeveria*

Pg 34-39: Zantedeschia, Calla Lily

Pg 40: *Tulipa,* Tulip

Pg 41: *Leucadendron* species, Cone Bush

Pg 42: *Gazania*, African Daisy

Pg 45: *Echinacea purpurea,* Coneflower

Pg 46: *Gerbera,* Transvaal Daisy

Pg 48: *Anagallis arvensis,* Scarlet Pimpernel

Pg 49: *Ornithogalum dubium,* Star of Bethlehem

Pg 51: *Lillium* species

Pg 52: *Tulipa,* Tulip

Pg 53: *Zantedeschia,* Calla Lily

Pg 55: *Echinacea*, Coneflower

Pg 56: *Anagallis arvensis,* Scarlet Pimpernel

Pg 58: *Papaver nudicaule,* Iceland Poppy

Pg 61-63: *Papaver nudicaule*, Iceland Poppy

Pg 65: Cotyledon succulent species

Pg 66: *Papaver nudicaule*, Iceland poppy

Pg 67: *Anagallis arvensis*, pimpernel

Pg 68: *Tulipa,* Tulip

Pg 71: *Ornithogalum dubium*, Star of Bethlehem

Pg 72: *Anagallis arvensis,* Scarlet Pimpernel

Pg 74: *Lilium* species, Lily

Pg 75: *Tulipa,* Tulip

Pg 79: *Echinacea,* Coneflower

Pg 81, 82: *Zantedeschia,* Calla Lily

Pg 84: *Zantedeschia,* Calla Lily

Pg 85: Lilium species

Pg 86: *Papaver nudicaule,* Iceland poppy

Pg 88: *Hellebores,* Lenton rose

Pg 89: Dahlia species

Pg 91: *Papaver nudicaule*, Iceland Poppy

Pg 93: *Anthurium* species

Pg 96: *Datura wrightii,* Sacred Datura

Pg 99: *Tulipa,* Tulip

Pg 101: *Agapanthus africanus,* Lily of the Nile

Pg 103: *Ipomoea*, Morning Glory

Pg 104: Dahlia species

Pg 105: Daisy species

Pg 107-109: *Ipomoea,* Morning Glory

Pg 110: Geranium species, Crainesbill

Pg 111, 112: *Agapanthus africanus,* Lily of the Nile

Pg 115: Phlox

Pg 116: Cactus species

Pg 117: *Graptopetalum* species

Pg 118, 119: *Agapanthus africanus*, Lily of the Nile

Pg 120: *Zantedeschia*, Calla Lilly

Pg 121: *Agapanthus africanus*, Agapanthus

Pg 125: *Sisyrinchium bellum,* Western Blue-eyed grass

Pg 126, 127: *Iris x hollandica,* Dutch iris "Blue Diamond"

ACKNOWLEDGMENTS

Special thanks to my good friend and mentor David Hume Kennerly. Without him this book would not have happened. It never hurts to have a Pulitzer Prize winning photographer on your side. David got this book going and has been there for me every step of the way.

Who knew I'd ever ask a pollination ecologist to write something for me? I got the best. Stephen Buchmann wrote the excellent foreword, and put the birds, the bees, and the flowers into perspective.

I would also like to thank Patricia Z. Smith not only for her poetry, but her encouragement. Patricia also managed to write the beautiful words here as she was creating two books of her own.

Aaron Landworth of Garden Concierge in Malibu, California supplied the scientific and common names for the book. Thanks for your valuable contribution.

Tom Walker brilliantly designed *An Affair of Flowers*. I'm particularly pleased with his cover idea, it visually launched this project.

Special thanks to Kirby Anderson, Managing Editor at ORO Editions, for stepping in and taking charge when the project stalled, getting us to the finish line.

A big-shout out to Gordon Goff, the publisher of ORO Editions, for believing in my art. I'll be back at him with another book idea after this one comes out!